CW00409177

THE CULTUI HAN~ ~~~~~

An essential Australian guide

David Grogan
Colin Mercer
with David Engwicht

Allen & Unwin
In association with Arts Queensland & the Australia Council

ARTS QUEENSLAND

Australia Council
for the Arts

Major sponsor:
The Queensland Office of
Arts and Cultural
Development.

Publication assisted by the
Australia Council, the Federal
Government's arts funding and
advisory body.

First published in 1995
Allen & Unwin Pty Ltd
9 Atchison Street, St Leonards, NSW 2065 Australia

National Library of Australia
Cataloguing-in-publication entry:
Grogan, David.
   The cultural planning handbook: an essential Australian guide.
   ISBN 1 86373 894 0.
   1. Community art projects—Australia. 2. Arts surveys—Australia. 3.
   Australia—Cultural policy. I. Mercer, Colin. II. Queensland Office of
   Arts and Cultural Development. III. Australia Council. IV. Title.
306.40994

Set in 10/14.5 Zapf Calligraphic 801 by David Engwicht Consultancy

10 9 8 7 6 5 4 3 2 1

Contents

Foreword

The *Cultural Planning Handbook: An essential Australian guide* has been two years in the making and has engaged the talents of some of Australia's leading cultural professionals. It was commissioned by *Arts Queensland* and the *Australia Council* in 1993 in recognition of the growing importance of cultural planning across the three levels of government—Commonwealth, state and local. Perhaps more importantly, it was commissioned and published in order to fill the information gap about the subject of cultural planning itself.

When you go to a library today, a search under the key words 'cultural planning—Australia' will not yield many texts, if any. When an administrator at local government level, an engineer, or an elected official wants to know more about planning for the quality of life of their community, there are few texts readily available in the bookstores to explain both the precepts and potentials of the enterprise on which they are embarking.

This handbook will provide readers with an overview of what cultural planning is all about. It will give professionals direction in conducting cultural planning at the local government level and will help communities come to terms with the breadth of any cultural planning project. As the authors explain more fully, **the most important part of cultural planning is the process of coming to know the culture of your community**—a process referred to in this guide as 'cultural assessment' and often referred to elsewhere as 'cultural mapping'. Once people are aware of, and appreciate, the cultural resources in their community—both in their tangible and intangible aspects—integrated planning to maintain and enhance quality of life becomes possible.

Given the inherent value of cultural resources for both the social and economic health of our communities, we can only be surprised at how long it has taken to document the task of cultural planning in the manner of this volume. This handbook provides readers with a framework to plan for the strategic development of their community's culture. It suggests means to arrive at, and prioritise objectives and strategies for cultural development. As importantly, it encourages and assists readers to conduct these tasks in community contexts and with community involvement.

When it comes to cultural planning, the authors suggest, community engagement in the process from the outset may well prove to be the most essential element if success is to be achieved in the long term. This reflects shifts in public policy in many Western countries, where there is a growing recognition of the importance of a community's ownership of, and engagement with, their own cultural, social and economic futures.

The *Cultural Planning Handbook* is not intended to be the 'last word' on cultural planning. Planners will need to consult more widely as their tasks become more specifically directed to the development of particular types of cultural resources. While internationally there are very few guides to cultural planning available which will provide the kind of overview presented here, information is now available in relation to individual aspects of cultural planning such as cultural industry development, cultural heritage management, consultative processes, exemplary projects and so on. To assist reader in finding their way 'through the cultural planning maze', details of a number of texts and other resource material useful for the Australian situation are provided in the handbook's bibliography.

Australia is currently acknowledged to be one of the world's most successful managers of multiculturalism. Many international visitors are now making the long trek to our shores to experience our distinctive 'Aussie' character and diversity of lifestyles as well as our unique environment. Across all regions of Australia, government authorities are realising the opportunities that this diversity and distinctiveness present and are endeavouring to manage these opportunities. What are the things that make our culture work best for us locally, regionally and as a nation? How best can we manage our distinctive and abundant cultural resources?

Australia has long been recognised as rich in its natural endowment. Perhaps because they are so easily taken for granted, we are only just becoming aware that we are rich in cultural resources as well. This handbook seeks to provide the tools for governments and communities to enrich their cultural resources.

1 Introduction

Who is this handbook for?
What will it help you do?
What will be the final product?
Why have a cultural plan?
How long will it take?

The Mayor of Bulla-Bulla had ignored calls for a cultural development plan... one week too long. But that is to get ahead of the story.

1ntroduction

Cultural planning is a relatively new field. Local authorities are coming under increasing pressure to get involved in cultural planning as community groups and business interests begin to understand the economic and livability benefits of cultural planning. Many progressive councils now view cultural planning as essential core business—as important as roads, rates and rubbish. Many see cultural planning as a valuable tool for achieving integrated local area planning.

Who is this handbook for?

This handbook is a practical tool for helping local authorities evolve a cultural development strategy. It will therefore be of primary interest to:
- local authority officials
- planning professionals (all disciplines)
- tourism-based businesses
- civic-minded citizens
- arts and cultural industries.

The handbook contains detailed, step-by-step instructions which a project manager, steering committee and small team of workers (with average levels of skill and experience in planning and community work) should be able to follow with a minimum of outside assistance. The first two chapters will also serve to provide lay readers with an overview of the nature and benefits of cultural planning.

What will it help you do?

This handbook will guide you through a *process* of:

* reaching a common understanding of the importance of cultural planning to economic and community life
* assessing your current cultural resources
* creating a community vision for the future
* devising a strategy to take you to your preferred future
* implementing the strategy.

What will be the final product?

The final product is a cultural development action plan, which when implemented should:

* improve quality of life through improving the availability, diversity and quality of cultural resources
* improve equity in access to cultural resources
* create a more robust and vital local and regional economy
* coordinate cultural activities
* lead to a better utilisation and coordination of scarce local government resources
* create a framework for professional development for those individuals or groups wishing to make a career in the arts and cultural industries.

Why have a cultural plan?

Cultural development enables people to feel that they belong in a community—a community which has a distinctive personality and identity. In this context, culture and the arts have two very important and simultaneous roles to play in the broad areas of *economic development* and *social development*. Cultural policy can be viewed as a 'mediator' between the profit and efficiency objectives of economic policy and the human development, access and participation objectives of a social policy.

Economic advantages

On his 1990 visit to Brisbane, Robert McNulty, the President of the US organisation *Partners for Livable Communities*, suggested that every level of government should have an agency that corresponds to a 'Ministry for the Quality of Life'. He proposed that the major concerns of such an agency should be the arts, culture, leisure and entertainment activities and all those things that add to the attractiveness and quality of amenity in a particular community. He argued that due to advances in telecommunications and transport, companies are not so limited when choosing where to establish their operations. 'Quality of life' may be the most important consideration for many of these businesses. Those cities, towns or regions with the greatest livability will gain an economic advantage due to shifting priorities for companies making locational choices.

Turnover in the arts and cultural industries in Australia amounts to around $20 billion per annum with value added around $9 billion. On the most recent figures this was the second fastest growth sector for employment. The cultural industries comprise not only traditional arts and crafts, but also the print and electronic media, including: publishing; film; television and video-production; graphic art and design; the leisure and recreation sectors; music and advertising. Cultural planning can lead to imaginative new strategies for local economic development in this growing industry sector.

Tourism

Culture and the arts have a strategic role to play in the dynamic environmental/cultural tourism industry. Many national and international indicators suggest that tourists are increasingly less interested in 'showpiece' resorts and destinations and more interested in environmental, cultural, heritage, ethnic and historical features. Cultural tourism is a strategy designed to satisfy the requirements of economic development in an industry which now represents 6% of the nation's GDP—without sacrificing environmental and cultural quality.

Given the importance of tourism to Australia's current and future economic development, and the notorious vacillations of the existing industry, cultural tourism may provide some elements of stability beyond the transient fads of theme parks, resorts and luxury complexes. It may also have the spin-off benefit of improving the quantity and quality of local cultural resources.

While fishing with his son, Cr Jones had a flash of inspiration. What Bulla-Bulla needed was a cultural development plan. He would raise the matter at the next council meeting.

Social and community development

Cultural resources play a fundamental role in all those elements that create a sense of 'community'—individual affirmation, identity, communication between individuals and between groups, participation, and a sense of place. Management of cultural resources is also intimately linked to the issues of social justice and community development. These issues should be seen as integral—rather than as marginal or supplementary—to cultural development.

The availability and quality of cultural resources can determine whether or not people think their area is a 'good place to live'. The goal of a cultural development strategy is to manage and improve these resources.

Integrated local area planning

State and federal governments are placing an increasing emphasis on the integration of planning at the local level in order to tailor services and planning to the particular needs of each community, and in order to avoid duplication between the various levels of government. Cultural planning, as outlined in this handbook, is seen as one tool for achieving integrated planning at the local level. All planning and activity—whether at government, business or private levels—has cultural and social impacts. Cultural planning provides a holistic framework in which those working in different disciplines can grasp the 'big picture'.

How long will it take?

Developing a cultural plan may take as long as you choose, depending on the resources available, what areas you wish to cover in your plan, to what depth you want to cover them, and the size of the community you are planning for. The process suggested here will typically take from 12 to 18 months.

There may be instances where plans have been prepared in substantially less time than this, but building a sense of community ownership through good consultation often takes longer and is ultimately more successful. It must also be recognised that because the cultural activities that normally take place in your community will continue, people will only have a limited amount of time to contribute to the planning processes outlined. It is also likely that other strategic planning exercises will be underway, each of them making demands on people's time. Each community will have a pace that it feels comfortable with, and this should dictate the duration of the process, not some artificially imposed deadline.

2 Setting the scene

What is culture?

What are cultural resources?

What is cultural assessment?

What is cultural development?

How does it fit with other strategic planning?

Why is local government a key player in cultural planning?

Who should we involve?

Getting started

Summary of recommended methodology

Not everyone in Bulla-Bulla was convinced of the need for a cultural development strategy. Some suffered from cultural blindness.

Setting the scene

Most people and communities suffer from 'cultural blindness'. Ask them about the culture of their town or city and they are likely to respond: *'What culture? We don't have a culture.'* This cultural blindness is understandable. We grow up with the things that make our place and our way of life different. To us they are the norm. To the tourists or visitors they are unique. They may have come halfway around the world just to experience our unique architecture, topography, history, customs and the way we conduct our everyday life. It is these things that form our distinctive *culture*. Just as we are fascinated by other people's cultures, they are fascinated by ours.

What is culture?

An outside-work gang at the Maroochy Shire Council defined culture as *'the personality of a particular place'*. A truck driver defined it as *'lifestyle'* and a grader operator described it as *'a way of life'* (Engwicht 1993: pp.15,16). Our culture is the unique combination of the place where we live and the people—the topography, the vegetation, the architecture, the monuments, history and the residents' customs, dress, ways of interacting, etc. As the *Creative Councils* report puts it:

11

> Our culture is everything that contributes to the quality of
> our lives. Going to the football is a cultural activity. Sitting at
> home knitting is a cultural activity. So is going to the pub,
> riding on a bus, watching the news, tinkering in the garage
> and pruning the roses. All of these things contribute to our
> way of life. Culture is a term that defines all the aspects
> which add up to our quality of life as individuals. We are all
> 'cultured'. Aspects both unique, and shared with other
> places, contribute to a community's culture. For all of us,
> culture is one of the basic things which makes life worth
> living. It gives our lives meaning and enjoyment. (Donovan
> 1993: p.3)

Ironically, part of many people's culture is the mistaken belief that
they have no culture.

Culture—not just the opera

Something of the breadth of culture can be appreciated by considering just three of the major elements of culture. Firstly, there is the
invisible *mind-set* which shapes every culture—the mythologies, beliefs, and values which determine people's way of life: their social
customs; methods and content of communications; their architecture,
streetscapes, and public buildings; and their forms of art. Secondly,
there are the *mediums* used to express culture—for example; art, lit-
erature, newspapers, television, architecture, urban design, informal
conversation, and formal meetings. Thirdly, there are the *artefacts*
produced by a culture—houses, streetscapes, cooking utensils, books,
institutions, sculptures, public buildings, etc. All three elements are
intimately interconnected and are part of what we refer to as 'culture'.

Culture does not simply mean *the arts*. It includes the arts—traditional, folk and new—and also a much wider range of human, physical, intellectual and spiritual activities, experiences, and forms. The
cultural life of a community is not just about a few people going to
the opera. It is about participation, celebration, identity, belonging to
a community and having a sense of place.

What are cultural resources?

A cultural resource is anything that contributes to the culture of a particular place or people. It may be something tangible—a heritage building, a civic centre, or seats in the main street. Or it may be intangible—a strong feeling of 'place', or attitudes of cooperation and tolerance between different cultural sub-groups. Cultural resources include the arts as traditionally defined, and also a much wider range of human and infrastructure resources. These include:

- The visual, performing and literary arts—skills and practices
- The contemporary cultural industries of film, video, broadcasting, photography, electronic music, publishing, design and fashion and the training institutions associated with them
- Specialist crafts such as jewellery, ceramics, and metal forging
- The structures and skills for managing, developing, distributing and marketing of arts, crafts and cultural industries products
- The quality, diversity and vitality of community life as reflected in:
  - cultural facilities such as libraries, museums, art galleries
  - performing arts venues, community centres
  - retailing, leisure, recreation and entertainment facilities
  - the attractiveness and accessibility of streets, public spaces and the built form
  - local traditions of sociability
  - festivals, fairs, etc.
- The positive presence of ethnic and cultural diversity
- Historical, artistic, archaeological and anthropological heritage, including local and introduced folk traditions and the ancient but still dynamically evolving resources of Aboriginal and Torres Strait Islander cultures
- Humanly created landscapes, amenities and features such as park systems, waterfronts, bora rings, streetscapes, and town squares
- External 'image' perceived by visitors and internal perceptions— the sense of 'identity' perceived by the local residents.

What is cultural assessment?

Cultural assessment is a cultural resources stocktake. An inventory of some resources is best collected via *quantitative* methods using existing databases, census data, and surveys. This guide recommends creating the following 'cultural resource profiles':

• General population profile
• Ethnic and indigenous population profile
• Arts/artists profile
• Existing cultural facilities profile
• Potential cultural facilities profile
• Education and youth activities profile
• Tourism and leisure activities profile
• Built, natural and community heritage profile
• Arts-related business profile
• Cultural industry profile.

Councillor Jones was engrossed in The Cultural Planning Handbook *when suddenly two anthropologists from the 21st century asked if they could do a cultural assessment of Bulla-Bulla. Fortunately he knew what they were talking about.*

Other cultural resources are best assessed by *qualitative* methods, or what is referred to in this guide as 'perceptual mapping'. A wide range of methods are used to map people's perceptions of:

• cultural groupings
• the spirit of the place
• cultural mind-sets
• cultural artefacts and their messages
• livability resources and corrosives
• accessibility.

Community cultural assessment or 'cultural mapping' is the process of identification and charting of cultural resources in the local area, with a view to modifying negative elements and enhancing positive elements in order to improve quality of life through economic, social and community development.

The base-line questions are:

• What cultural resources exist in a local community and are recognised as such?
• What cultural resources are there but aren't recognised?
• What cultural resources might be there with encouragement and planning?
• To what uses, in terms of individual and community development, can each of these resources be put?

The processes of mapping and assessment are necessarily community-based. Community involvement in charting cultural resources is part of the community development process. Some of these resources will have been taken for granted. Communities may not even be aware they already possess some of these resources. The assessment, therefore, enables a community to develop a stronger sense of identity and empowerment. In more technical terms, it is a process of community 'action research', with results being logged at every stage.

What is cultural development?

Cultural development is modifying the negative elements of a culture and enhancing the positive elements in order to improve quality of life. Just some of the elements of cultural development may be:

Community individuation

A sense of identity—knowing who you are and what makes you unique—is essential for the psychological wellbeing of both individuals and communities. It is also increasingly important economically. For example, tourists (particularly cultural tourists) are looking for 'an experience' that is an encounter with something that is different to what they experience at home. The stronger the personality and character of an area, the more likely it is to benefit from cultural tourism. Similarly, business people are attracted to places with high livability, which includes a strong sense of individuality. Cultural development can identify and strengthen this sense of identity.

Self-expression and internal dialogue

Cultural development is not just individuality—but also *expressing* one's identity. This can involve increasing people's access to the widest range of communication media in order for them to participate in expressing their identity and culture. It also means having the opportunities and forums in which to debate and discuss the nature of community culture and the areas in which it should change. Healthy internal dialogue between the cultural sub-groupings in the community promotes critical reflection and stimulates creativity. The culture of a people can only develop to the degree that diversity is nourished and the cross-fertilisation of ideas is encouraged.

Creating a sense of place

A sense of place is a discernable quality of some environments. We instinctively know when it is absent—places that feel like they belong to no-one. And we instinctively know when it is present—a people's square or a small creek where we go to read and reflect. This sense of place is no accident. It is the combination of numerous factors: the way the space connects us to the past, to other people, to the immediate environment, etc. It is partly to do with urban design, that is building setbacks, width of streets, orientation and design of public seating, landscaping, water, and art. For example, Portland USA requires all public car-parks in the city centre to have shops on the ground floor in recognition of the importance of continuity in the streetscape in improving a sense of place. This sense of place is also partly to do with local customs and patterns of social interaction. It is partly to do with transportation—method and speed of movement. Cultural development draws all these strands together and enhances this sense of place.

Feeding creativity

If a society is to survive and prosper, it must adapt to changing conditions. Adaption requires creativity, the act of bringing previously unconnected elements into a new relationship. Cultural development provides both the means and the opportunities for the cross-fertilisation of ideas. It provides a climate that stimulates creativity. This is not just through the formalised channels for expressing new ideas such as books, sculptures, gallery spaces, and performances. The design of public places and the way people live in and use their cities and towns can inhibit or encourage spontaneous exchanges of information and the debate of new ideas. It is no accident that some cities and towns have stronger traditions of innovation and creativity. Over the years they have cultivated their 'creative wealth'.

Inventing the future

A cultural development strategy is the sign of a community inventing its own future—a creative act. It is that same community evaluating its strengths, weaknesses, and the opportunities and threats (SWOT analysis) and deciding how it will get to its desired future.

How does it fit with other strategic planning?

State and local governments are increasingly required to prepare strategic plans for a wide range of activities, all of which impact on local communities and their quality of life. It is increasingly necessary that these strategies are integrated with each other, to avoid conflicting outcomes and in order to achieve economies of scale and coordination.

No matter what areas are addressed by the different strategic plans, they all share a number of characteristics in common. Each strategy must:

- be based on high quality, well-analysed data
- be aimed at an agreed vision of how the community want their area to be in the future
- recognise and mobilise existing and potential linkages between itself and all other strategies. (See figure 2.1.)

Recognising these linkages between strategic planning areas is important. For example, the planning and development of cultural resources is now seen as central to local government policy agendas in economic, infrastructural and social development. There is a need, then, to start with a broad definition and categorisation of cultural resources in order to broaden the agenda beyond the arts as traditionally defined and to make the necessary connections between these diverse resources in a strategic framework.

The processes outlined in this guide have been designed to produce a cultural development strategy plan that is capable of being implemented at a local authority level with the same degree of confidence and authority as any other strategic plan. The process includes high-quality research and information gathering; detailed strategy formulation, evaluation and implementation; and robust public participation at every step. It also incorporates the means of reviewing

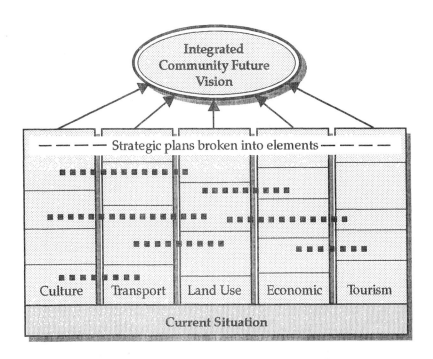

Fig. 2.1 The links between the different elements of strategic plans can be mapped. All strategic plans are based on helping communities achieve their future visions.

the organisational structure and corporate culture of the council, ensuring that the strategy is not bypassed or inappropriately over-ruled by other priorities. Through these means, cultural planning and development can be treated as an integral part of the local planning process, integrated with statutory and strategic planning, corporate planning and all associated policies, frameworks and documents.

Why is local government a key player in cultural planning?

Local government is the form of government which is closest to people's everyday lives and experiences. Every action of local government has an impact on local culture—from the placement of trees and street furniture to the maintenance, public profile and use of heritage buildings; from the design of new developments to the impacts of new roads on the culture and integrity of communities. These decisions, together with the relationship between communities and their council, are what determine the shape of people's living environment—its texture and dynamics.

Sporting activities, festivals, museums, art galleries, performance venues, restaurants and shopping malls are also, to one degree or another, within the jurisdiction of local government. These are not just services which are to be provided but fundamental activities, sites and institutions which determine the quality of the experience of living in or visiting a community.

Since the early 1970s, local government has been assuming a greater profile in the Australian political process and this profile is sure to increase in the coming years. This has been especially true in the area of human services and community development. The 1987 *Report of the Office of Local Government* in the then Department of Local Government and Administrative Services stated in its first recommendation that: 'Local government [is] a natural and effective vehicle for community development initiatives and for human service programmes which adopt a community development approach.'

Some local government councils have tended to see community development as a rather passive and peripheral 'welfare' activity. The reality is that for all local governments, the core activity is *already* community development—whether the local government authority likes it or not. Roads, rates and rubbish are a means to an end: the establishment, servicing and development of communities.

Pressure on councils by state and federal governments to establish community and cultural development strategic plans can be viewed as an attempt to encourage local government to have a much more sophisticated and realistic understanding of the role they are already playing. These plans should effectively assist both government and communities. For communities the plans should provide recognition of the distinctive needs and desires of the different cultural groupings in the community, and encourage grassroots participation. For the local authority, the plans legitimise and promote the roles of facilitation, liaison, research, planning, coordination of services and project management. This should bring communities and local authorities into a closer partnership involving forms of active consultation and participation, both formal and informal.

Cr Jones thought it might be a good point in the council meeting to raise the need for a cultural development strategy. Little did he know that, while he didn't get the support he expected from his fellow councillors, a public meeting on the other side of town decided they had waited one week too long.

To consolidate these embryonic elements of effective partnership between government and the community requires some imaginative thinking. Local government, of course, has a special role as a provider of services and as a funding authority, but there are other functions which need to be taken into account in cultural planning. These include the roles for local government outlined by Jean Roberts (1989: pp. 45, 46):

- *Facilitator:* where local government provides various support functions to community organisations. This support can take the form of land or premises, equipment, financial assistance and administrative support.

- *Catalyst and initiator:* where local government initiates or jointly develops services and programs with community groups.

- *Point of liaison and advocacy:* where local government acts on behalf of the community to other levels of government to ensure adequate resourcing of community needs through grants and other forms of provision.

- *Researcher and planner:* in the development of a local planning framework in consultation with the community.

- *Coordinator of services:* providing a link between community, different elements of local government and non-government organisations.

- *Project manager:* where expertise and resources are provided to encourage forms of community development and self-reliance

- *Information and promotional agency:* where the resources of local government are used to advertise programs, services and initiatives widely and imaginatively.

- *Networker:* where local government develops a network of community organisations and other government agencies providing both information and 'brokerage' services.

Local government is already being called upon to do all of these things, and it is within this range of activities that cultural planning can help to provide direction and purpose.

Who should we involve?

Identifying the stakeholders

Stakeholders can be divided into the three general categories of government, community and private sector. They can also be classified as *general* stakeholders or *operational* stakeholders. A general stakeholder may be a group such as youth or an ethnic group while an operational stakeholder provides cultural services or is involved in activities which impact on the quality or quantity of cultural resources. Stakeholders include funding or support agencies and a broad cross-section of your community. If cultural planning is to be successful locally, it must take into account all community sectors—from the large businesses to the elderly and the unemployed. This will ensure that the unique character of your community is recognised and developed in the planning process.

Here is a list of possible stakeholders to get you started. The titles of the departments change from time to time and state to state so you will need to check out your local scene and add to the list according to your particular circumstances.

Federal government
- Department of Communication and the Arts
- The Australia Council
- Aboriginal and Torres Strait Islander Commission (ATSIC)
- Office of Multicultural Affairs (OMA)
- Department of Employment, Education and Training (DEET)
- Department of Human Services and Health (DHSH)

State government
- Office of Arts and Cultural Development
- Department of Housing Local Government & Planning
- Health Department
- Family Services Department

- Aboriginal & Torres Strait Islander Affairs Department
- Environment Department
- Heritage Department

Community
- Arts and crafts organisations
- Heritage organisations and historical societies
- Ratepayers and progress associations
- Ethnic groups and cultural associations
- Aboriginal and Torres Strait Islander organisations
- Community development and service organisations
- Senior citizens organisations
- Youth organisations
- Local chapters of planning associations (architects, engineers, urban planners, etc.)
- Prominent local people.

Private sector
- Tourism-related businesses
- Arts/crafts related businesses
- Heritage-related businesses
- Leisure-related businesses
- Restaurants and cafes
- Local media (newspapers, television, radio).

There are countless examples of strategic plans which have remained on the shelves without ever getting close to implementation. This may be for economic or political reasons. Or it may simply be that the process of planning has not been sufficiently open to allow community stakeholders to be persuaded that the strategy is necessary. Many projects need community momentum to help push them into the implementation stage. It is very important, therefore, to treat the *process* of planning as at least equal to the final product— the plan itself. If, during the production of the plan, you have not negotiated the end product with a sufficient range of stakeholders, it

is likely that the end product will be ignored or campaigned against. If you haven't got the elected representatives, government officers, key community organisations and individuals, and representatives of the private sector onboard during the process then you may not have sufficient consensus on the viability of the final product. If you haven't made the connections in the consultation and planning process between the interests of those concerned with economic development, with the built and natural environments, and with social and community development, then you have achieved only a sectoral rather than a strategic cultural plan.

Cultural organisations

To secure both initial and ongoing commitment, you will need to persuade those stakeholders 'at the coal face'—cultural organisations—that the strategy is in their interest. How do you achieve this?

It is in the interest of cultural organisations, traditionally short of resources, to increase the potential for revenue generation, to raise their profile through publicity, lobbying and advocacy, to strengthen their management structures, to gain access to facilities and to increase audiences for their products and services. A cultural development strategy should be able to address all of these needs by:

- Identifying new sources of funding, support and revenue generation
- Raising the public profile of cultural organisations and activities
- Enabling cultural organisations to participate in strategic management and financial planning
- Identifying existing and potential facilities for display, performance and production
- Enabling cultural organisations to improve their existing products and identify new products
- Enabling cultural organisations to identify new audiences and improve access to their products.

Getting started

Outside consultants or in-house

This handbook has been designed to help an in-house team undertake a cultural development strategy. The local authority may decide to call in outside experts to undertake particular tasks, or to manage the entire process. The allocation of tasks, to a large extent, will depend on budgets, personnel, and their availability. It is suggested that if you are using outside consultants, they be given the opportunity to contribute their ideas on the best methodology. As cultural development is a relatively new field, new understanding and methodologies are constantly being tested.

'Expert' or 'community-based' approach

One of the first choices open to the council is whether to use internal or external experts to undertake the necessary investigations and planning processes, or to adopt a community-based approach, or some combination of the two. The expert approach may involve the council using specialist consultants or the council may have expert staff who can prepare the assessment and strategy in-house. The expert approach is often typified by less consultation and more decisions being taken by people with specific skills and experience in cultural planning. This may suit some councils as it is often less expensive and quicker than other processes with more extensive community involvement. Although they may be initially less expensive, these fast-track methods of strategic planning may be less cost effective because the resultant strategies lack the necessary community support required for implementation.

A composite approach may involve the use of experts for certain elements of the process, with the community participating to a greater or lesser degree. Communities will vary in their level of experience and have access to different levels of expertise to assist them in this process. Although this manual could be used to evolve a cultural development strategy with minimal community consultation, it has been designed primarily to assist those wishing to take the community approach.

Steering committee

Normally, the first step is for the local authority to appoint a steering committee to oversee the production of the cultural development strategy, which may take 12 to 18 months, depending on the size of the area, the complexity of the issues and the expertise and resources available. It is recommended that, from the outset, the steering committee also views its role as including the implemention of the strategy, or at least ensuring that the mechanisms for implementing the strategy are in place—for example, appointment of a properly resourced, full-time cultural development officer.

Appointment of the steering committee is a vital and sensitive stage of the process, which can either make or break the success of the entire project. The local authority needs the wholehearted support of the community if the processes outlined in this handbook are to function properly. It cannot therefore simply appoint whoever it wants to the steering committee and expect it to work. Neither should it put a notice in the local paper, hold a public meeting and appoint a committee from among those who happen to turn up on the night. It may turn out OK, but more often than not it won't.

Remember that this process may have a significant impact on your community's cultural, social and even economic life. The steering committee will play the important role of ensuring that your community's cultural resources are identified and used strategically to achieve broader community goals.

Some councils may already have in place a community consultation committee or forum which could serve as the steering committee, such as, in Queensland, the *Regional Arts Development Committees*. In the event that there is no such body in existence, the following process has been designed to assist in the process of identifying appropriate committee members. Rather than risk offending, omitting or getting groups or key individuals offside at the outset, the local authority should appoint a councillor who has some knowledge and understanding of cultural issues to establish the steering committee. The council's chosen representative should have sufficient political skills to build a steering committee that is representative, effective and keen to do the job.

The councillor should assemble a contact list of cultural organisations and key individuals in the community and invite these people to participate. It is particularly important to get the first contact correct as some groups may perceive the whole process as alien, unnecessary or potentially intrusive. In compiling the contact list, the councillor should identify people who can liaise with those groups in order to have an invitation for the group to participate in the process delivered appropriately. The list should include arts and crafts organisations, Aboriginal and Torres Strait Islander organisations, ethnic or religious groups, historical societies, tourism and cultural businesses, literary and music groups, contemporary film and video producers etc. The list may be long and varied, but should reflect as completely as possible the many facets of your community's cultural life.

Where personal contact is appropriate, the councillor and the identified liaison person from a group may need to attend a meeting with the group to explain what the cultural development process is about and how the outcomes will be used. The group may need some time to consider this information and may seek clarification before they decide whether to participate. This process may take longer with some groups, particularly Aboriginal and Torres Strait Islander groups, those from non-English speaking backgrounds and groups which may feel threatened by changes inherent in the process. Such groups should not be pressured into unrealistically tight timeframes. They may require several visits/discussions and ask for information to be provided/interpreted in ways they find appropriate. This process may take several weeks, or in some circumstances, even several months.

It may be appropriate to make contingency plans based on some groups not being ready to participate. This could involve deciding to prepare a strategy which does not include issues relating to specific groups and possibly encouraging the group or groups to produce their own plan at a later date. These negotiations require sensitivity and respect for other people's rights and positions.

A public meeting should then be called to elect the steering committee. All groups and key individuals, especially those interested in nominating a member to the steering committee, should be invited by mail or phone. Notices giving details of the purpose, location and timing of the meeting should also be placed in the local media.

Large committees can embrace a wider range of representative views, but tend to become unwieldy for decision making. A committee of seven to ten members is considered a reasonable size. If greater representation is considered appropriate, consideration could be given to a two-tiered structure, with a smaller executive and a larger advisory group or several working parties on specific issues.

The mix of committee members should take into account the following:

- Range of arts, cultural and business organisations in your area
- Representation for groups with special circumstances or needs
- Balance of gender, age, experience and cultural backgrounds
- Level of commitment and availability to stick at the task over a period of at least 12 months.

A suggested agenda for this meeting to elect a steering group is:

- Introduction and thanks for attending—Mayor
- Format and objectives of meeting
- Background to cultural development strategy and broad goals
- Presentation which explains the process of cultural planning (a range of resources is available—see Appendix C)
- Questions of clarification and group discussion
- Draft proposal for steering committee
- Recommended size (tiered?)
- Organisations/areas which might be represented
- Getting the balance right
- Nomination of potential members
- Discussion
- Voting (if necessary)
- Closure and thanks.

The members of the steering committee should arrange to meet soon after the initial meeting to elect office bearers. The composition of the steering committee will vary according to local circumstances, but typically should include:

- Chairperson who is eminent in some form of artistic or cultural endeavour within the local community and who has the experience, commitment and interpersonal skills necessary to successfully lead the process
- Deputy Chairperson, Secretary and Treasurer
- The responsible councillor (who may fill one of the above roles)

- Sufficient other members to adequately reflect your community's cultural life.

Project manager

The first major task of the steering committee is to identify and appoint a suitable project manager to have overall responsibility for the process on a day-to-day basis. The project manager should generally report to a monthly meeting of the steering committee. This person should have, or be capable of quickly acquiring, an appropriate combination of skills, experience and personal qualities. These include:

- Skills
  - Strategic planning
  - Project management/scheduling
  - Report writing
  - Meeting procedures.

- Experience
  - Background in arts or cultural organisation
  - Preparation of strategic or policy plans
  - Management of large, multi disciplinary projects
  - Market research
  - Community consultation

- Personal Qualities
  - Good interpersonal skills
  - Organisational ability
  - Ability to communicate with people from different cultural backgrounds and widely divergent interests
  - Able to lead by example and keep others to an agreed timetable and direction.

The decision as to who fills this role will depend on the size and complexity of the task. The project manager for a rural area with a smaller population could be an unpaid volunteer working in a part-time capacity. Some councils may have an officer who could be assigned this task in addition to their normal duties. In areas which have large and culturally diverse communities, it may be feasible to appoint an appropriately qualified contractor or consultant to manage some or all of the process.

It is recognised that there are not many people who already have the ideal combination of skills and experience and are available to undertake this task. Appoint the best person you can, within budgetary and resource constraints, and organise some appropriate training. This can be provided by private trainers and arts and cultural training bodies. Your state government arts and cultural department should be able to inform you what training or backup materials are available. (*Places not spaces: placemaking in Australia* (Winikoff, 1995) contains a detailed listing of training resources and contact organisations. See Appendix C for more details.)

Flexibility

Once the project manager has been appointed, the steering committee should review the suggested program of activities in this handbook and map a provisional course of activities. Depending on local conditions and circumstances, some stages may be irrelevant and others may need to be added. It is important, when deciding the provisional course of action, to keep in mind the objectives of each activity and to ask the crucial question: 'how will this activity enable the evolution of our cultural development strategy?' For example, it may be decided that while some information would be interesting, it may absorb a lot of energy and contribute little to the overall process.

The course of action is provisional for a very good reason. Room needs to be left for responses to what is discovered at each phase of the project. This may mean adding activities and dropping or modifying others. Flexibility and tactical responsiveness to local conditions are crucial in the process. The processes suggested here are more of a 'tool box' rather than a 'blueprint'.

Community awareness

The project manager and the steering committee will need to make important decisions about how best to communicate with all community groups. This handbook provides a core process of meetings and workshops which may alienate or be difficult to understand for some community members. Your local media, community organisations and government agencies which have a community service function will be able to provide you with important advice on community sectors that may need special or individual attention if they are to be encouraged to participate.

An estimated timetable of the various steps involved should be prepared and publicised at the outset. This can be amended progressively, particularly if more time is required for consultation. Attempting to implement the process at a faster rate than the community can absorb is to invite disaster. Indicative timelines are shown in the program overview, figure 2.2.

Although the mechanisms will vary from place to place, each steering committee is strongly advised to develop their own specific media and public relations strategies, including provisions for print and electronic media, posters, newsletters, competitions and informal information networks. This process should be initiated before the next public meeting and be designed to increase attendance and subsequent active participation. Publicity should contain the following:

- The aims of the process
- Anticipated benefits
- Opportunities for participation
- Progress to date.

Those responsible for managing and facilitating community cultural resources have a special role to play in information and publicity strategies. It is part of the nature of cultural forms—the nature of words, images, symbols, performances, gestures, rituals—to *say something*. From graffiti to urban design to youth fashion and music, 'culture never stops talking. It is a flexible and multifaceted information system in its own right and so offers a continuous forum and domain for messages and information.

Cultural forms and activities therefore offer immense potential in communicating the meaning of a community and its community life both to its residents and visitors. The means range from the headline status of roadside hoardings to the more discreet statements contained in art objects, street furniture or monuments. A community cultural planning process should make the most of the communicative power of cultural forms to 'sell' the process.

Summary of recommended methodology

A summary of the steps in the recommended methodology are contained in fig. 2.2

To others it was just a sculpture. But to Cr Jones it was a central plank in his strategy to convince council. He understood the communicative power of the cultural artefact.

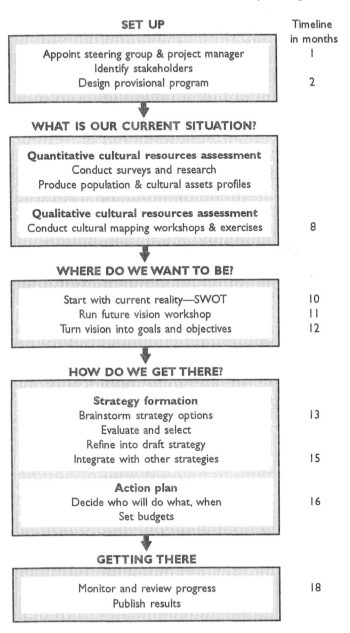

SET UP

Timeline
in months

Appoint steering group & project manager — 1
Identify stakeholders
Design provisional program — 2

WHAT IS OUR CURRENT SITUATION?

Quantitative cultural resources assessment
Conduct surveys and research
Produce population & cultural assets profiles

Qualitative cultural resources assessment
Conduct cultural mapping workshops & exercises — 8

WHERE DO WE WANT TO BE?

Start with current reality—SWOT — 10
Run future vision workshop — 11
Turn vision into goals and objectives — 12

HOW DO WE GET THERE?

Strategy formation
Brainstorm strategy options — 13
Evaluate and select
Refine into draft strategy
Integrate with other strategies — 15

Action plan
Decide who will do what, when — 16
Set budgets

GETTING THERE

Monitor and review progress — 18
Publish results

Fig. 2.2 Overview of methodology to produce cultural development plan and possible timeline

The strategy will seek answers to the following questions:

- Who are the stakeholders and the participants in the cultural life of our community and what do these people think of the current situation and what would they like changed?
- How will the differences in interest and personality types among the stakeholders affect the process of cultural strategic planning, and how can recognition of these differences be harnessed to improve the process and result in a more vibrant and diverse outcome?
- What vision should be guiding our cultural development strategy?
- How can we identify, document and retain the cultural factors which contribute positively to the quality of life within our community?
- Which groups within our community experience barriers to participation in cultural activities, and how can these be removed?
- How can we link our process to other planning exercises within our local area, region or area of cultural activity?
- What strengths, weaknesses, threats and opportunities related to cultural resources and activities can we identify in our area?
- What strategies and plans can we devise to take advantage of the strengths and opportunities? How can we remedy or minimise weaknesses and threats?
- How can we be sure that the mix of projects, programs, activities and plans that comprise our strategy are the best ones; that adequate financial and human resources will be available and that the necessary political and community commitment can be maintained for implementation of the strategy?
- What ongoing resources and support will be available to community groups participating in the implementation of the strategy? How will progress be monitored?

3 Quantitative cultural assessment

The survey and data collection process

Population profile

Cultural assets and activities profile

Policy audit

Quantitative data analysis and publication

Cr Jones started the assessment stage of the study with a family shot outside the council chambers. The concept of cultural diversity came to him in a blinding flash. The people of Bulla-Bulla liked different cheeses.

Quantitative cultural assessment

All good strategies are based on a strong understanding of current reality. The assessment of cultural resources uses both quantitative and qualitative processes. This chapter deals with the former and the next chapter deals with the latter. The collection of data for the quantitative assessment should be seen as an integral part of the consultation process—even when examining Australian Bureau of Statistics data. Such research helps to supplement and fill out the picture that will be provided by residents. It is simply not possible to talk to everyone in a community. This is why consultation always needs to be backed up by more detailed statistical research.

The survey and data collection process

Survey and data-collection teams

The most labour-intensive part of the process is the survey and data collection stage. To cope with the workload, you may wish to consider forming a number of working parties. To conduct the surveys listed in figure 3.1 within the sensible timeframe of approximately six months may require between seven and fifteen survey teams. The final number will be decided by the number of helpers available,

Potential grouping	Survey Area

Population profiles

Population demographics
People with disabilities
Older people
Non-English speaking background
Aboriginal and Torres Strait Islander

Artsworkers

Cultural assets profile

Public facilities
Cultural business

Aboriginal and Torres Strait Islander culture

Heritage/environment
Cultural organisations
Cultural education and training resources

Cultural and environmental tourism
Festivals and events

Religious organisations
Ethnic media and activities
Cuisine

Figure 3.1 Potential groupings of survey tasks for survey teams

the size of each task and the resources available to manage the teams. A potentially arrangement of groupings is shown in figure 3.1.

Some councils may be in a position to use consultants or research organisations to collect primary research data. The advantage is that this may increase the reliability and validity of the survey results and decrease the timeframe if experienced and well-trained professional interviewers and supervisors are used. The disadvantages are: the high cost; lack of local knowledge; and the missed opportunity of engendering commitment to the process by involving local people early in the data collection and analysis stages. The alternative is to train volunteers from the community, especially from cultural organisations, to undertake the various surveys. Local schools, colleges and universities may be a useful resource in this work.

To obtain sufficient volunteers/participants for these working parties, the steering committee may have to hold a meeting of interested people from the community, outline the task involved and ask for assistance. The meeting should be planned four to six weeks in advance. The steering committee should make out a list of all known arts and cultural organisations in the area and prepare letters asking those organisations to notify their members of the meeting, including date and time, venue, background to the cultural planning process, purpose of the meeting and expected outcomes.

In addition to local organisations, national or state organisations also have databases which include artsworkers, cultural educators or people with historical or cultural interests. Although they are unlikely to simply give you the names and addresses of the people in your study area, they may be prepared to send a notice to people on their lists. Such organisations include arts councils, crafts councils, the National Trust, the Community Arts Networks, the National Association of the Visual Arts and other arts and cultural service organisations in the region or state.

Press releases should be sent to all local radio, television and print media as well as publishers of newsletters and relevant magazines. Paid advertisements should be inserted in the most appropriate papers in the final week before the meeting. Posters and leaflets may also be used.

A suggested agenda for this meeting is:
• Introduction and thanks for attending
• Format and objectives of meeting

- Background to cultural development strategy and the provisional program of activities
- Outline need for data collection, how the data will be used, how it fits in total program
- Discuss survey process and need for assistance with various working parties
- Circulate attendance sheets and ask people to indicate the areas and capacities in which they would be prepared to assist
- Break into survey team working groups, select a team leader, organise and set date for first meeting
- Closure and thanks.

Following the public meeting, the project manager and team leaders should meet to organise team orientation and training. To save reinventing the wheel, ask around to see what survey forms have been used by other local authorities and what commercial products are available. Groups which choose to develop their own survey component will need to build their own questionnaires. This process is described below, however more comprehensive manuals on designing and carrying out surveys are available, for example:

- *Planning healthy communities—a guide to doing community needs assessment* - Community Health Research Unit, 1991, Flinders Press
- *Guide to community needs assessment*—Office of Local Government, 1988, Australian Government Publishing Service
- *A guide to Australian social statistics*—Australian Bureau of Statistics, 1992, ABS

Survey design

Surveys can be conducted as a *sampling*—a randomly chosen and statistically significant percentage of the total population of interest—or as a *census*—everyone in the population of interest. Census may be used where there are smaller areas or where it is considered important to capture information about everybody (for example, every artsworker or every historic site).

For a sample survey to be useful as a reasonably factual basis for strategic planning, it should be randomly selected from a known list of potential respondents. As the surveys outlined below are designed largely to explore and record the presence of as yet unknown populations of artsworkers, historic sites, cultural organisations etc., most are census-style surveys. Groups wishing to undertake sample surveys may refer to the three publications cited above.

Is your Survey User friendly?

Once the decision is made on whether it is to be a sample survey or census, the method of collecting the data needs to be decided—face-to-face interviews, telephone interviews, mail or distributed surveys. The strengths and weaknesses of each of these approaches are summarised in figure 3.2.

Utilising existing databases and collections

Each team should begin by gathering as much existing information as possible about the populations and resources to be surveyed. This may include accessing commercial mailing lists, marketing information and club membership information on individuals and organisations, and databases listing sites and facilities.

Due to privacy considerations, managers of some databases may be unwilling to provide names and information without the consent of those involved. In such cases, they may be prepared to simply give an indication of the number of individuals on their database from your area, perhaps broken down into different categories.

Estimating the numbers to be surveyed

Each survey team has to estimate the number of people, organisations or sites which will need to be included in their surveys. This is

Method	Advantages	Disadvantages
Face-to-face	• High response rate • Interviewer able to interpret questionnaire and assist respondent • Ensure all questions answered • Increased accuracy	• Highest cost • Time consuming • Not good for large populations • Possibility of bias due to interaction between respondent and interviewer
Telephone	• Most flexible • Lowest cost • Fast • Interviewer able to explain questions • High response and accuracy • Reduces variability of bias compared with face-to-face	• Does not include people without phones or those with unlisted numbers • Respondent does not have copy of questionnaire to assist in understanding topic • Length and complexity of questionnaire is limited
Mail	• Low cost • Questionnaire may be relatively long and complex • Response rates can be increased by good covering letter and follow-up	• Low response rates • Inaccurate and incomplete answers • No assistance to interpret (unles phone help line provided) • Long time to get good response rate
Distributed	• Moderate cost • Can enlist help of organisation to induce members to respond • Can get good economies of scale if filled in at meeting— allows explanations • Moderate responses if members prompted by their organisations	• Relatively low response rate • Long time

Figure 3.2 Comparison of survey methods

necessary for estimating the number of interviewers, the number of questionnaire forms that need to be printed and how long the survey process will take. It is also necessary from a statistical point of view because you have to keep trying for a response until at least two-thirds of all the questionnaires that were sent out have been properly filled in and returned. This process of estimating can be simplified by the following process:

- Convene a meeting of a number of people who are familiar with the population which is to be surveyed. For example, for the artsworker survey, ask office bearers from the local arts, dance, drama, music and writing groups
- Ask them to bring membership lists, printouts of databases etc. to the meeting
- On a large sheet of butcher's paper, draw up a matrix divided into rows and columns with the columns representing the main suburbs or districts and the rows representing subgroups in the community to be surveyed—for example, artsworkers may be divided into the main types of art forms
- Use this as the master list and write people's names in the respective boxes. If there are too many names or the names are unknown, place ticks or estimated numbers in the box
- Ask other people to comment and add names and make estimates as the list grows.

Obtaining cooperation from the people to be surveyed

All reasonable steps to maximise the response rate and accuracy of the surveys should be taken. These could include:

- Create a name and logo for the cultural development strategy and use it on all communications and promotions
- Send press releases and place advertisements in all local media informing the public of the survey process
- With all questionnaires include a covering letter, signed by the Mayor, and a background information sheet

- Provide official identification for all interviewers
- Obtain active support of all cultural organisations and ensure participation by their members
- Wherever possible, ensure that interviews are carried out by appointment and explanation of purpose be given in advance
- Keep the process to an agreed timetable
- Keep the demands on people's time to a minimum.

Timetabling

Once the number of survey teams has been established, the project manager should prepare a timetable for the survey and data gathering stage. Depending on who is doing what, it should be possible to get quite a few of the different surveys going simultaneously. This will shorten the total time it takes to get all the base information together. A condensed timetable could take better advantage of interest which might be created by any publicity and media exposure. The time taken to collect the necessary information may take from three to six months.

Coding and quality control

If you are designing and using your own questionnaires you will have to consider how the information is to be recorded and how you will code and monitor the data entry. To enable easier, more reliable coding and data entry, and to facilitate subsequent interpretation of the data, you should try to maximise the proportion of your questions which are in a 'closed' format. Closed format questions are where you supply a range of possible answers and ask the respondent to choose the one which best fits their circumstances.

Questions can vary in type and complexity. Here are some examples and an explanation of their strengths and weaknesses.

    1. Please state your sex ☐ male ☐ female

This is a typical closed question with only two responses possible.

When entering data, a 'no response' category is necessary.

> 2. How often do you attend classes?
>   Every day   ☐
>   Once or twice a week ☐
>   Occasionally   ☐
>   Never   ☐

This closed question is more complex than question one, but the responses are still mutually exclusive and cover all possibilities.

> 3. How satisfied are you with the current services your family receives from the council?

	Very Dissatisfied	Dis- satisfied	Don't know/ Don't care	Satisfied	Very Satisfied
Youth activities	☐	☐	☐	☐	☐
Aged support	☐	☐	☐	☐	☐
Public transport	☐	☐	☐	☐	☐

This is a simple Likert or rating scale. You can use 3, 5, 7 or 9 categories according to how much detail you require. This is a structured way of analysing how people feel about any issue or topic.

> 4. What is your group's main type of activity?
>   Visual art   ☐
>   Pottery   ☐
>   Sculpture   ☐
>   Installation art   ☐
>   Other   ☐ please specify.............................

This is the most difficult type of closed question and is used to probe issues that have many possible responses. To use this type of question properly you must already have a reasonable knowledge of the range of possible responses and be able to put these into categories. It also needs an *Other—please specify* category. If the number of categories is too small you will get an unacceptably high number of respondents using the *Other* option. If the number of categories is too large, it diminishes the power of analysis. This type of question is very useful for many of the cultural resource survey areas. This means that the questionnaires will require relatively more care in the design and pilot testing stages, but this may be time well spent when it comes to analysing the data and preparing profiles.

5. Please state your main training needs—you may select up to three categories (in the relevant box, write *1* for your main priority, *2* for your second and *3* for your third)

Marketing   ☐
Book-keeping   ☐
Budgeting   ☐
Design   ☐
Database administration   ☐
Credit control   ☐
Sales techniques   ☐

This is a closed, multiple choice format which gives flexibility and indicates people's preferences. The drawback is that it requires a higher level of computer programming to sort the data and it is harder to interpret the results.

6. What type of facilities are required in your area?
....
....
....

This is a typical open-ended (as opposed to closed) question. It requires the least amount of planning, but yields a large amount of information which is more difficult to analyse. Responses can be forced into categories subsequently, but this requires that all responses be read, summarised, the summaries aggregated into categories, then all forms re-coded.

Data entry and reporting

Many questionnaire forms will have missing responses. Decide whether information gaps can be tolerated, or the form returned for completion or discarded. To achieve quality control, it is essential to scrutinise each form prior to data entry.

Sophisticated databases have inbuilt error trapping coded into the software, so the program does 'smart' checking of data as it is entered to ensure that the information conforms to appropriate specifications. Quality control is still required to ensure that the information on the forms is accurate and complete.

Depending on the number of forms, you can use manual tallying of responses or enter the data into a standard computer spreadsheet. This will enable very basic interpretation such as: '47 of the 55 people surveyed answered question 6; 65% were in favour of

... *Data Entry* ....

the new cultural centre; 22% were against it; and 13% did not care if it proceeded or not'. If you wish to analyse questions in more detail (for example, if you want a breakdown of responses to question 6 by age, sex and suburb) or if the total number of forms becomes too large (most people find more than 100 very difficult to process manually) you need to use a database of some sort.

The usefulness of the cultural resources assessment data collection phase is only as good as the reports and profiles that are generated from it. The information needs to be presented clearly and simply with comments on what the data means, how it compares with other areas, whether the trends are going up or down and what are the strategic implications of the data.

Population profile

Purpose of profile

Prior to formulating policies or strategies on cultural development for your area, it is strongly recommended that a detailed population profile of your community be prepared and disseminated as part of your information and issues paper for workshop participants. Information about the number and type of different people living in your area may help the strategies to be more relevant and focused.

If there are other groups who have prepared, or are preparing other types of strategies—land use, economic development, social development, tourism, recreation, etc.—you may be able to reuse their information or collaborate with them in the preparation of a community profile. Government departments may also have up to date information which they have collected for planning purposes. For example the federal Department of Human Services and Health has prepared population profiles for local areas in many parts of Australia. While these are prepared from a health perspective, they may contain some useful information of a more general nature that could be included in your profile. Local council staff may be aware of recent planning work undertaken. Listed below are the details of what should be included in the population profile and how to collect the data where it is not already available as a result of other community planning processes.

General demographics

To construct a general population profile from census data, the first step is to obtain a copy of the *basic community profile* for your area from the Australian Bureau of Statistics. This has 57 tables, which is much more information than you need. The most relevant tables are:

- B01—Selected characteristics
- B03—State and statistical local area of usual residence 5 years ago

- B04—Aboriginality by sex
- B05—Age by sex
- B08—Birthplace (countries) by sex
- B10—Birthplace of mother and father
- B11—Language spoken at home by sex
- B13—Religion by sex
- B14—Type of educational institution attended (FT/PT) by sex
- B16—Qualification (highest) by sex
- B20—Age by labour force status (FT/PT) by sex.

You may also wish to browse through the other tables to see if any of the information is relevant to the preparation of a cultural development strategy for your area.

In addition to general population demographic information from the census, special surveys or research may be needed to obtain additional data on groups with special needs within the community—particularly the groups targeted in government equity programs, including:

- Women
- Aboriginals and Torres Strait Islanders
- People with a non-English speaking background
- People with disabilities
- Older people
- Youth.

Women

The census and other ABS publications can reveal lots of information about women at the local level. Most of the tables with information about individuals include figures for both men and women, allowing researchers to develop a separate profile of the female population. This profile can then be compared to profiles for the entire Australian population or to profiles of other groups in your community. This comparison shows how typical the women in your area may be and could indicate how policies need to be developed to assist them in participating more fully in cultural life.

The women's profile can include:

- Age
- Income
- Labour force participation, industry, occupation and employment status
- Ethnicity, religion and language background
- Education, health and family details.

This information can be used to determine potential demand or access barriers and indicate priorities for programs and activities to encourage equitable participation.

Information may also be available from other bodies such as state government departments and universities. For example, Arts Queensland is undertaking a research project *Women in the Arts and Cultural Industries in Queensland* (1994). It may also be worth reading how public policy and the shape of urban environments can disenfranchise women.

The above process can be applied to building a profile for all the groups listed below.

Aboriginals and Torres Strait Islanders

The census contains some information on Aboriginals and Torres Strait Islanders in each local community. Additional information is available through the Aboriginal and Torres Strait Islander Commission (ATSIC) in Canberra and the relevant department in each state and territory government. In some areas, there are also strong local formal and informal associations, including statutory Land Councils. All these bodies may be able to contribute information and analyses for the preparation of Aboriginal and Torres Strait Islander profiles.

It is strongly recommend that any work on such profiles, and any subsequent survey, should be undertaken by members of the Aboriginal and Torres Strait Islander community themselves, with such assistance as they request. This will help avoid cross-cultural confusion or misinterpretation.

Non-English speaking background

As with the Aboriginal and Torres Strait Islander population, it is greatly preferable if people from non-English speaking backgrounds can be responsible for the development of profiles for their community or communities. Their history and traditions are, in many parts of Australia, the dominant feature. This information is vital to the development of an appropriate cultural development strategy for such communities.

People with disabilities

The task of collecting information on people with disabilities is made difficult by the multiplicity of agencies dealing with different types of disability and the incidence of people with multiple or borderline disability types that do not fit easily into standard schemes of classification. The broadest classifications for people with disabilities are: intellectual, psychological, physical, and sensory. Additional details can be added according to the age of the person or the degree of severity of the disability. The name, location and services offered by agencies involved in supporting people with disabilities may also be collected.

Older people

Information about people in retirement age brackets (60–65 years or older) can be obtained through the most recent census and an annual ABS publication on estimated resident population. To develop a meaningful profile of older people in your community, you need to collect extra information about their circumstances, activities and services available to them, particularly focusing on opportunities to participate in cultural activities. This additional information may include:

- Retirement villages
- Nursing homes and hostels

- Home care and nursing services
- Day respite and community centres
- Seniors clubs and social activities.

Youth

Youth constitute one of the most important and vibrant groups in the cultural life of any community. Separate profiles should be compiled for the following groups:

- Pre-school children
- School children
- Teenagers
- Early twenties.

In addition to educational activities, young people may be involved in a wide range of formal groups, clubs and associations or may participate on an informal, individual basis in different artistic, social or cultural activities. The formal activities and levels of participation for young people can be obtained from the various organising bodies.

Young people may also be involved in a range of activities which have no formal organisation but are still readily identifiable. Graffiti, rock bands, rap and even gathering in the local shops are youth cultural activities which deserve attention in your community cultural assessment. Local police and community workers will point you to youth activities which are perceived as a community problem and which you may wish to address with appropriate cultural strategies.

What is usually overlooked in reviewing youth cultural activities are cultural activities for children—particularly patterns of play. Paul Tranter (1993), in an important Australian study on children's independent mobility, documents how changes in society have impacted on children's play patterns and their experience of place. It may be important not only to construct a profile of children's play and recreational activities, but if possible, to map how these patterns have changed over time. Any long-term cultural development strategy must have the developmental needs of children as a central focus.

Artsworkers

If one of the primary goals of your cultural development strategy is to increase the contribution of the arts and cultural industries to your local economy, then artsworkers are key stakeholders. And an important task of information collection prior to the needs assessment and strategy formulation stages is a survey of all artsworkers in your area. This can be a time consuming and painstaking task, as not all artsworkers can be contacted through cultural organisations, and many may be difficult to locate.

An *artsworker* can be defined as a person who, in the last two years, has been actively involved in some form of artistic/creative or cultural activity. Useful categorisations of artsworkers are:

* Full-time professional—those spending more than 35 hours per week engaged in their artwork
* Part-time professional—those spending less than 35 hours per week engaged in their artwork
* Leisure—those who have other major sources of income and who do not wish to be considered as professional artsworkers.

The amount of remuneration is not considered generally to be an indication of 'professionalism'. Arts Queensland, for example, describes a professional artist as someone who:

* Identifies themselves as a professional on the basis of skill, training or experience
* Is accepted by peers as professional
* May or may not earn income from artwork.

The base information which may be required from the survey includes:

* Name, address and contact details
* Information which correlates to the community's demographic profile, including age, sex, etc.—to enable comparisons with the most recent census profile for the area
* Areas of expertise

- Background information as to their experience, qualifications and achievements
- Their ability and willingness to teach in various art forms may also assist in subsequent strategy formulation.

Some artsworkers may be cynical or distrustful of planning processes and the motives they perceive behind them. Considerable effort may need to be put into explaining the benefits of cultural industry development. A useful analogy would be to refer to the state

The whole council huddled in silent expectation. This was a proud moment for Cr Jones—the unwrapping of the population profiles.

of the tourism industry in Australia 20 years ago. At that time, tourism was characterised by:

- Many small unsophisticated operations—mainly family run motels and cafes
- Low turnover
- A focus on local markets, with little marketing
- No united industry voice or organisational structure
- No career path for young people entering the industry
- Limited curricula/institutions for vocational training.

This situation, which is similar to the current state of cultural industries, has changed dramatically over the last 20 years. Although many artsworkers would not wish to be compared to the tourism industry, the analogy illustrates the *process* of industry-building which is beginning to affect a wide range of cultural and artistic areas. Artsworkers, through the cultural development strategy process, can seize the initiative, control their agenda, and work through the process in an informed and co-operative manner.

Information from the artsworker survey is designed to be used in several ways.

- Prepare the artsworker profile.
- Provide basic facts and figures for the people involved in the process of drawing up strategies which affect artsworkers.
- Improve the process of consultation—you have to know who the artsworkers are to be able to talk to them.
- Coordinate subsequent training, networking and marketing exercises—you need to know which artsworkers are interested in various topics, markets and activities.

The artsworker profile should be short (around 2 pages) and should describe the types of artsworkers found in the area, their demographic characteristics, and the way they see themselves as working people. The profile should also include a description of the range and quality of the artsworkers' output expressed in their own terms.

Cultural assets and activities profile

Public facilities

Collection of a complete set of data about public facilities used by your community for cultural purposes is an essential part of the data collection exercise. This information will be used to design policies about the type and location of facilities which will be required. If other groups in your area are preparing social or recreation strategies, they may require the same information. Coordination and sharing of information with these groups could save time and money. The types of facilities on which information is required are:

- Specialised facilities, such as galleries, museums, libraries, theatres etc.
- Multi purpose facilities, such as halls, community centres, showgrounds etc.
- Open air facilities, such as malls, concert shells etc.

Details of how they are managed, how often they are used and what they are used for could also be collected. This information should be presented in a public facilities profile.

Cultural businesses

One of the main objectives of the cultural development strategy process may be to identify just how large and important the cultural sector is in the context of the local or regional economy. This may be an essential part of convincing governments and the private sector that supporting arts and cultural industries is worthwhile for economic and job creation reasons, as well as for the social and community benefits they bring.

A large number of cultural business types and corresponding occupations have been defined as part of the Australian Bureau of Statistics' *Culture-Leisure Industry Statistical Framework* and the *Australian Standard Classification of Occupations*. Reference may be made to these frameworks (obtainable through your state's Australian Bureau of Statistics office) in drawing up a list of cultural businesses to be surveyed. You should also contact your local economic development board, or its equivalent, to determine how much information already exists on these enterprises and to what extent you can save time and money by cooperating with other bodies interested in sharing this information.

Fixed heritage

One of the features which most clearly differentiates one area from all others is its unique history, historical sites, heritage buildings and local character. To date, only a fraction of the national estate has been documented on federal and state registers (collective lists of these assets which are deemed to have national significance). The cultural development strategy process provides an opportunity for communities to document their fixed heritage assets and to integrate this knowledge with plans for future community development.

The types of heritage assets which need to be identified and recorded include:

- The names (including former or other names) and locations of sites of local historical importance
- Tenure and type of custodial arrangements or ownership
- The nature of the asset (ruins, building, other structure)
- Summary of features, including protection status.

The starting points for creating this inventory should be existing collections and information held by local museums, historical societies and heritage interest groups. To enable comparison between information collected locally and that held by government departments, the established criteria for describing and recording historic sites and heritage buildings should be adopted.

The heritage profile should describe the area's history and cultural roots. It should highlight the types and conditions of its most noteworthy heritage assets.

Movable heritage/material culture

Most local authorities have some form of museum and art collection, either within the council or run by a separate association. These have traditionally taken the form of a small museum or gallery, many of which are under-resourced for conservation of the artefacts in their possession.

An alternative approach, which does not involve acquisition, housing and management of a collection, is the concept of a 'distributed collection'. All the relevant details needed to care for objects in a gallery or museum are collected, but the artefacts are left where they are found. Alternatively, a range of museum collections can be managed on a regional or even on a national basis—allowing resource sharing and opening up new opportunities for touring and display.

The details to be collected in the movable heritage and material culture profile include:

- Location
- Description
- Condition
- Ownership
- Provenance
- Conditions relating to access.

Aboriginal and Torres Strait Islander cultures

Indigenous communities have a unique place in Australian cultural development. They represent and manifest the continent's oldest cultural traditions with a distinctive heritage in both material and spiritual terms. In traditional arts and crafts—as in areas of contemporary design, fashion, film, television and music production—indigenous culture is enjoying an unprecedented national and international profile. Further, for indigenous communities the arts and culture are not separable and isolated domains of activity: they are *integral* to the whole life patterns and experiences of these communities.

There are very real dangers of an exploitative, superficial and ultimately short-term approach to indigenous cultural resources if they are treated simply as objects to be viewed by 'external' communities (the 'OK, here are the tourists, now dance' approach). Progress in securing these communities a greater degree of economic self-reliance may involve incentives for revenue generating ventures, training initiatives and infrastructure development. If indigenous cultural resources are to become vital to the overall cultural profile of a community, the following principles need to be borne in mind:

- Community initiation and ownership of cultural development projects
- The right to negotiate the terms of access to sacred sites, keeping places and other areas of special cultural significance
- The right of indigenous communities to establish the terms of reference for negotiation and consultation.

There are special conditions and provisos attached to the assessment and mapping of cultural resources in Aboriginal and Torres Strait Islander communities. As with non-indigenous communities, it is crucial that the community have ownership of the process and conduct it on their own terms. Indigenous communities are rightly suspicious of surveys, questionnaires and people with clipboards. The manner in which any assessment is conducted will need to be determined by the cultural protocol appropriate to each community. Indigenous communities, in the tradition of oral cultures, place a great deal of emphasis on systematic, detailed and wide-ranging oral consultation. The process of consultation within Aboriginal and Torres Strait Islander communities may therefore take much longer than is customary in non-indigenous communities. This consultation, protracted as it may be, is crucial to the survey process if the diversity, complexity, historical, social and spiritual wealth of the region's indigenous communities are to be recognised and tapped.

A good place to start in informing and involving Aboriginal and Torres Strait Islander communities in your cultural assessment process is to talk with service providers who have already established solid working relationships based on trust and mutual respect. Once informed of the process, the communities themselves must be free to establish their own cultural visions and objectives and to document their own cultural resources. Overall cultural development strategies can then be developed to facilitate these visions and objectives and make connections with broader community goals and activities.

Cultural organisations

The cultural development strategy process has the potential of bringing all the separate cultural organisations within the community together, working towards a shared vision and common goal. An essential prerequisite, therefore, is to prepare an inventory of all cultural organisations. The inventory should include:

- Name and corporate status of organisation
- Contact details
- Information about the organisation's objectives, membership and budget.

Although not as important as the information listed above, some councils may also find it useful to gather information about each group's accommodation status. This could be useful when considering multi-user facility strategies at some later point in time.

Religious institutions

Religion has historically played an important role in community life and the development of cultural identity and social values. Information for the religious component of the profile can be obtained from the latest census and from a survey of religious institutions. The survey can provide additional data on active membership, range of services and activities, objectives and programs, resources and premises, employment and related details. Important connections can be made between the objectives and resources of religious groups and the community's broader cultural vision.

Cultural education and training resources

Central to the whole cultural development process is the concept of each community determining its own needs, what it wants to do, what it currently does and how well it does it. Strategies for growth and improvement need to be supported by programs of education, training and skills development. To identify your area's capacity in these areas, you need to undertake a survey of educational and training resources for cultural industries. This should include both private and public resources. The type of information which may be obtained includes:

- Name and type of institution
- Contact details
- Types of tuition offered including any qualifications granted
- Areas of cultural tuition
- Course content and details.

Cultural and environmental tourism

One of the fastest growing sectors of the national tourism market is cultural/environmental tourism, where visitors seek to experience firsthand an area's natural wonders or to understand the way of life of a local area or region. The cultural component can include: interpretation of a region's industrial base, for example wine making, ginger factory or cattle station; Aboriginal Torres Strait Islander culture; ethnic culture; festivals such as Sydney's Gay and Lesbian Mardi Gras or the Maleny Folk Festival; local architecture; courses and workshops such as summer art schools or cooking classes; cultural museums such as the Longreach Stockmans' Hall of Fame; or simply doing what is seen as typically Australian such as having a drink in a pub.

As the physical environment often forms a strong part of local culture, it is both compatible and intertwined with cultural tourism. Both aspects may rely on a tour guide or self-explanatory framework/ theme to help the traveller interpret the environment. True cultural and environmental tourism seeks an authentic experience borne out of understanding and respect for the environmental and cultural attributes of those places and societies being visited. Information which may be used to develop a profile in this area includes:

- Name of attraction/operation
- Contact details
- Type of operations and area of interest
- Corporate details including staff, experience, turnover, etc.
- Interpretive materials available
- Other details about operations.

Festivals and events

Festivals and events can be major attracters of tourists and serve economic ends. They can also serve community development goals, helping communities to express their identity, and they also serve social needs, allowing people to 'let off steam' in socially acceptable ways and within a supportive environment. Events cover a wide range of organised community or commercial activities and can include sporting events such as the Olympic Games or World Cup Soccer tournaments, expositions such as the six month long World Expos, down to commercial or cultural events of local significance only.

In *The Festivals Review* undertaken recently for Arts Queensland, author Roberta Bonnin (1993: p.3) defined a festival as:

> A unique occasion when people come together for a lively series of special events, activities and experiences, delivered with a clear purpose, concentrated in time, and celebrating a community's appreciation of their arts, heritage, culture, spirit or place.

Festivals and events provide opportunities for artsworkers to sell their products and promote their talents, and they provide communities with opportunities to reaffirm and display their cultural heritage. They can attract large numbers of participants and visitors, providing opportunities for economic development, particularly those held in rural and remote areas and those held on a regular basis.

Targeting and scheduling festivals and events can be a problem for organisers, as information about the nature, timing and location of other events is often difficult to obtain. One outcome of a cultural development strategy may be designing and maintaining a calendar of festivals and events and/or publishing information about their objectives and the contribution they make to cultural and economic development.

This information would typically include:

- Name and location of festival/event
- Contact details
- Management and corporate details
- Location/venue and timetable information
- Objectives
- Any special information which will allow better identification and comparison of festivals and events
- Staffing, attendance and turnover
- Other descriptive or promotional details.

NESB media and activities review

Australia is one of the world's most culturally diverse nations. Actual numbers of residents from Non-English speaking backgrounds (NESB) can be obtained from the most recent Australian Bureau of Statistics population census data. In addition to the demographic analysis, additional information on media usage and activities by various ethnic groups will assist in the recognition of the depth, vitality and diversity of local cultural identity.

The nature and degree of consumption of NESB print media will give a further indication of active links with people's cultural origins. This can be ascertained by a survey of the number and type of newspapers and magazines in languages other than English being sold through local outlets. These outlets can include newspaper shops, stores selling ethnic foods, clubs and community associations.

Information which can be recorded includes:

- Name of paper/magazine/radio station
- Publisher
- Nationality/region/cultural group of origin
- Format and content
- Release period and total circulation
- Number sold locally, estimated listener base.

Cuisine, cafes and restaurants

Although Australia has not developed regional cuisine to the same extent as Europe or Asia, the range and quality of dining experiences available is generally recognised as an indicator of an area's sophistication or cosmopolitanism. The range, quality and variety of restaurants and cafes is often an important indicator of, and catalyst for, a community's cultural diversity and vitality. Restaurants and cultural/entertainment activities have a close relationship. After-hours economies can prosper and the social life of the community can benefit when due attention is given to the importance of this relationship.

Despite the inherent difficulties, it is feasible to collect and evaluate the following types of information:

- Name and address of establishment
- Contact details
- Type
- Quality self-assessment
- Number of seats (covers)
- Other features.

Policy audit

You are assessing your cultural resources for a reason: to enable you to plan and develop them in order to improve quality of life. However, it is pointless to do this in ignorance of, and isolation from, relevant policy frameworks at local, regional, state and national levels.

There is always the possibility that you will commit time and resources to a wheel that has already been invented elsewhere. It is important, therefore, to be aware of the 'policy climate' and to be conscious of initiatives elsewhere in the locality, region, state and nation by undertaking a 'policy audit' of the relevant policy frameworks which might have implications for your initiative.

This can be difficult. Policies are often made on the run and the life span of many policy frameworks is less than three years. Nonetheless, a policy audit is always important to the process of community cultural assessment for two reasons:

- To identify *constraints* on your own initiative
- To identify *potentials* in support, funding and facilitation.

Given the changing contours of policy and the changing nature of the agencies which have responsibility for and carriage of these policies, it is only possible here to identify the relevant generic 'pigeon holes' which you will need to consider. These are taken from the commonwealth level to the local government level. In identifying policy frameworks which are relevant to your own initiative, it is important, in the first instance, to identify the relevant 'lead agencies'. At the Commonwealth level these may include:

- Department of Communications and the Arts (DoCA)
- Australian Cultural Development Office within DoCA
- Australia Council (a statutory authority which reports to DoCA)
- Department of Human Services and Health (DHSH)
- Department of Employment, Education and Training (DEET)
- Aboriginal and Torres Strait Islander Commission (ATSIC)
- Office of Multicultural Affairs (OMA).

Each state has a department of arts and cultural development. Each state will also have departments looking after tourism, sport and recreation and local government. All departments and agencies are actively involved in cultural planning and may be a valuable source of information about relevant policy frameworks.

Technically every policy framework of every department and authority has *some* impact on local culture, that is, people's way of life. To audit all of these policy frameworks will be beyond the resources of most local authorities. Some research—and a few telephone calls—will quickly identify which are most relevant to your own objectives. Department of Commuications and the Arts, for example, is responsible for programs and policies in arts, cultural heritage and development.

Cr Jones' hunch proved correct. After a hard dig, he found that Bulla-Bulla Shire Council was indeed sitting on a cultural assets goldmine.

Quantitative data analysis and publication

Once each of the working parties has produced the relevant profiles, the data can be cross-referenced to further enrich the profiles. For example, the artsworker profile group may have already compared its data with the general population profile, but if it hasn't, a comparison may produce the following kinds of information:

- Although women make up half the population of our shire, and the average age is 32 years, 67% of artsworkers in the visual arts are women, and the average age of this group is 48 years
- 27% of the town's population is actively involved in either music, drama or visual arts.

Using these enriched profiles, a draft report or *information and issues paper* should be prepared presenting the results of your surveys and community research. This should be circulated for comment and discussion, with a suitable campaign informing the public and interested parties how they can access and respond to the contents. Copies could be placed in local libraries.

The information paper should include data from the surveys in the form of lists, tables and profiles. Lists should not include any personal details and should be used mainly to summarise the number, type and location of the various parameters surveyed. The numbers in each category should be shown both as raw numbers and as percentages of the total category (for example, total population, all cultural facilities etc.). Percentages are used to compare the distribution of items within different-sized populations and this is often a better indication of what is going on than the raw numbers.

A profile should be no more than one or two pages long and contain a mixture of descriptive text, statistics and analytical or interpretive comments. It should be comprehensive in its coverage, and where relevant, use comparisons.

The paper may include information from:

- Secondary research sources, such as the census or other reports
- The surveys (lists, tables and profiles)
- The policy framework analysis
- Any related results from the qualitative research (discussed in the next chapter).

After a month or so, submissions could be considered and this document revised into final format. It can then be released as a stand-alone publication, but could also ultimately be incorporated in the *Cultural development strategy* document as background and supporting material.

4 Qualitative cultural assessment

Cultural mapping
Mapping cultural groups
Mapping the 'spirit of place'
Mapping cultural mind-sets
Mapping artefacts and their messages
Livability resources and corrosives
Mapping access and access barriers
Charting coordination opportunities
Self-perception questionnaire/workshop
Using workshops
Documenting and displaying maps

Cr Jones was just about to plough his potato paddock when three lost Zephlines from Mars asked for his cultural maps. Cr Jones rang his secretary on the mobile phone and had her make two copies of each. As he ploughed on he mused; 'I wonder if Zephlines are as advanced as the Bulla-Bulla Council?'

4 Qualitative Cultural Assessment

The previous chapter explored quantitative methods of assessing your cultural resources. Quantitative assessment is the easiest for planners and decision makers to deal with—it is based on data that can be measured objectively. But culture is also about things that can't be measured easily: people's *experience* of their place and their community. This chapter suggests ways of getting a snap-shot of your non-quantifiable cultural resources and an indication of the *quality* of these resources.

Cultural mapping

Maps are representations of how people see the *relationships* of the various elements in an environment. Sometimes these maps are very literal, keeping everything to scale. In fact, many cultural planners would call the quantitative assessments outlined in the previous chapter 'cultural mapping'. Other times maps are based on perceptions and make no attempt at a literal or objective representation of reality. For example, in one cultural mapping exercise, children were asked to create maps of their neighbourhood. One child included a road close to home which took up most of the drawing. While this would appear a distortion of 'objective reality', it is nonetheless a true and accurate representation of the child's *perception* and *experience* of the road. The road was the boundary beyond which this child was not allowed to go—an uncrossable river of traffic which to them stretched to the horizon.

In explaining this difference in the way maps may be constructed—literal or symbolic—it must be underlined that even maps that appear to be an objective representation of reality are also perceptual maps. The drawer has made decisions about what will be included on the map: what are the important features; which elements are of less importance and will be left out. It is therefore a portrayal of what that person *perceives* as the elements that make that place special and noteworthy.

The term *cultural mapping*, as used in this chapter, is a way of understanding how people are experiencing their place and culture. This is important for a number of reasons. Often the 'things' that make a place special for people will not be picked up in a quantitative assessment—a tree by the creek where the kids of the neighbourhood meet, the diversity of ages in a neighbourhood, or the wildflowers outside the corner store. A quantitative assessment can tell you how many libraries there are, but it will not easily reveal *how* and to what extent they are contributing to the cultural and social life of the community. Nor does the quantitative assessment reveal those things that are missing or perceived as negatives—like the uncrossable road that stretches forever for the child.

Cultural mapping does not necessarily mean literal creation of maps on pieces of paper. 'Mapping' is any exercise that assists a community to express how they perceive and experience their community and environment. The rest of this chapter includes ideas for mapping under each of the suggested mapping areas. The methods you choose will depend on who is doing the mapping, availability and skills of facilitators, etc. We encourage you to be adventurous and invent your own mapping techniques. The methods you can use are as wide as the imagination.

Mapping cultural groups

What do we mean when we refer to a cultural group? Instinctively we think of an ethnic group—people who speak a different language or come from a different country. But a cultural group is any group in a society with a distinctive way of life. This way of life is based on a unique combination of beliefs, values, customs and relationships. In a country town, for example, the farmers may comprise a very different cultural group to those they refer to as 'the alternative life-stylers'. Women form a distinctive cultural group, as do children and people with disabilities. In fact, most people belong to a number of cultural groups which overlap. Even within a cultural group there may be distinctive subcultures.

It is not just the distinctive culture of each group which forms the culture of a place. It is also the way these groups relate to each other. While the quantitative analysis will give some clues as to which cultural groups exist in your community, it cannot explain the dynamic relationships between these cultural groups. Mapping can therefore take two forms. It can encourage people to express how they perceive themselves; or it can express how they relate to other cultural groupings.

Some ideas of how you can map the cultural groups in your community include:

- *Lists:* In small groups, have people make a list on butchers paper of all the cultural groups in the community. Ask them to place a coloured dot beside the groups they see themselves belonging to.
- *Mapping links:* Have individuals or small groups construct 'maps' by placing a circle around each of the cultural groups and then drawing links between the groups with words or images that depict the nature of the relationship. This can be done as an extension of the above activity or as a separate exercise.
- *Symbols:* Ask people to place on the map symbols, words or pictures which, to them, best sum up each of the cultural groups.

- *Interactive mapping:* Employ a community artist/facilitator to progressively construct the above map in a public place such as the main street, or alternatively have the map on a large mobile canvas that can be taken to groups such as schools, retirement villages, clubs, shopping centres, etc. The artist/facilitator asks people to identify which group/s they belong to, and if their group is not on the map to place it there. The artist/facilitator can then ask about symbols/words/images that characterise that group or their relationship to other groups. The respondent can be encouraged to place something directly onto the map, or be provided with materials to sketch or write their ideas which the artist adds later.

- *Mural 'tapestry':* A community artist can be employed to oversee the construction of a mural in a public place which depicts the various cultural groups in the community. Once the cultural groups to be represented have been decided, the artist can spend time with each, finding out what symbols and images best represent that group, weaving these into a 'tapestry' or mosaic.

One word of forewarning about mapping cultural groups. Those who belong to a dominant cultural grouping will often argue that they don't belong to a cultural group. Pushed, they may describe themselves as 'a typical member of the human race' or 'an average Australian'. When a woman or indigenous Australian or a person with a disability looks in the mirror, many are aware of those characteristics that make them different to the dominant cultural grouping. Those with the strongest sense of identity are those who perceive themselves as 'different'. Those who have travelled in a foreign country may have had this experience of being acutely aware that their identity has suddenly become defined by the areas in which they are different to the dominant cultural group. Travellers may even experience a strong sense of vulnerability. It is often difficult to get those in the dominant cultural groupings—particularly those whose decisions shape communities and their culture—to admit that their grouping has a distinctive culture, with distinctive beliefs and values.

Mapping the 'spirit of place'

What is it that gives your study area its personality and character? The following are just some methods of helping people express what is important to them.

- *Postcards.* Postcards try to capture the spirit of a place on a very small piece of card. Get people to imagine they are tourists in their own town or city and get them to make a postcard to send back to their relatives and friends. Provide them with magazines, photos of your area, pens, coloured paper, glue and an index type card. The postcards can then be mounted as a display. This can be run as a competition, and it works well in a workshop—particularly if people are expecting just another talk-fest.

- *Snapshots.* Get people to imagine that they are being forced to leave their town or city, knowing they will never be able to return. They take some snapshots to help preserve their memories of the place. Give them a disposable camera and ask them to go out and shoot the snapshots they would take. This can be run as a 'workshop' or as a competition. If run as a competition, people can use their own cameras, supplemented with the disposable cameras. Mount the results as an exhibition and have a *comments wall* where people can write their thoughts and responses. Small pieces of paper— perhaps headed *Penny for Your Thoughts*—can be provided, and when filled out, pinned on the wall. People love reading other people's comments and then responding to them.

- *Photo essay.* Invite two or three outside professional photographers (or community artists with photographic skills) to spend a few days each constructing a photographic essay which to them summaries the spirit of your place. It is important that these people are from a different place outside the community in question. They may identify distinctive characteristics that locals take for granted or consider to be the norm. The photo essay can be done as a separate exercise or in conjunction with the snap-shots exercise. Place the results in juxtaposition for more comments.

- *Chalk mural.* Have a 'This is [*your town/city*]' street or car-park party and hand out heaps of chalk. Encourage people to draw or write things which they think make your place special. Document people's contribution on film.
- *Fence painting.* A community artist can work with community groups in producing a fence painting or mural which summarises the spirit of your place.

Mapping cultural mind-sets

The one aspect of culture which is often ignored when doing a cultural assessment is the cultural mind-set—the invisible values, beliefs and mythologies which shape every aspect of culture. These

To Cr Jones' surprise, Kelvin, the shire engineer, had a large fold-out map in his head. Like newborn anthropologists, they combed every detail for clues to the culture of Bulla-Bulla. Cr Jones decided that what they discovered would make an interesting paper at the forthcoming Culture in Cities Conference.

values, beliefs and mythologies are incarnated into both social relationships and the built form. From examining the layout and artefacts of ancient villages or cities, anthropologists can make significant deductions about the culture of that place—how people related to each other, their beliefs, etc.

Why map these cultural mind-sets? Part of cultural development is promoting a greater level of understanding and tolerance of other cultural groupings. It is difficult to truly 'get inside the skin' of another cultural group unless you understand something of their values, beliefs and mythologies. It is particularly hard for decision makers and planners to create an equitable society if they are not aware of what is important to, and what motivates, the cultural groups to which they do not belong. Another aspect of cultural development is cultural groups enriching their own culture by integrating the positive aspects of other people's cultures into their own. In addition, cultural development involves communities recognising those elements of their culture which they should have outgrown. As children mature they outgrow some of the beliefs and values of their childhood. Mapping cultural mind-sets can be an opportunity for a community to mature by evaluating whether some aspects of its cultural mind-set need changing. For example, there may be agreement that the town feels inferior to a larger town just down the road, or that there are strong elements of racism or intolerance.

Mapping cultural mind-sets is the most difficult and sensitive of all the mapping exercises. Here are some ideas that may get you started:

- *Focus groups.* Convene focus groups with representatives from each of the cultural groupings identified. Start by asking them to list the things that are important to them as individuals and a group. Then ask them to examine *why* each of these things is important— the values, beliefs or mythologies that underlay them. This process may need skilled facilitation by someone who can coax people beyond superficial explanations.

important to them as a group and then to list the values, beliefs and mythologies that lay behind these. Then have each group report back, remaining in role. Immediately following each group's presentation, have the other groups, also staying in role, ask questions of clarification. The benefit of this approach is that it also teaches people how to 'get inside other people's skin' and appreciate their perspective. It is essential that there be a debriefing, best handled by a skilled facilitator, at the end of this process.

Cr Jones sat with a satisfied grin—his critics silenced. The seat from outside the council chambers had layed them in the aisles with her humour and insight. Wait till they heard how the rubbish bin intended to blow the whistle on the culture of Bulla-Bulla.

Mapping artefacts and their messages

Artefacts—books, cooking utensils, streets, public buildings, sculptures—are both the *expression* of culture and the *facilitator* of culture. Each of these conveys messages which are reflections of the cultural mind-set. Mapping artefacts and their messages is really turning residents into anthropologists who examine the architecture of the public buildings, the orientation of seating, streetscapes and monuments to discover something about their own culture. For example, one council examining the layout of the forecourt in front of their council chambers found that the doorway was hidden behind landscaping and that all the visual pathways in the court lead straight into the concrete pillars supporting the building. The architecture conveyed a strong message about the culture of the council. The design and use of artefacts is the 'body language' of a culture.

Examining artefacts and their messages is absolutely essential in improving a sense of place and making visitors feel welcome. Just as the architecture of the council chambers conveyed a particular message, the smallest elements of a place may combine in contradicting the sign on the city boundary which reads *'Welcome'*.

For those who find the mapping of cultural mind-sets too daunting, mapping artefacts and their messages is either a good first step or a partial substitute. The messages conveyed by the artefacts are messages about the cultural mind-set both past and present. Some ideas to get started:

- *Slide-kit.* The Australia Council and Community Arts Network has a slide kit entitled *Finding the Personality of Our Place* which teaches people skills in reading their culture from such things as the orientation of public seating. While produced initially as a training kit for the Maroochy Shire Council, it can be adapted by using some local slides.
- *Role-play.* Have people break into small groups and pick some artefact in town—rubbish bins, particular street, monument—and

write a dialogue with that artefact. The kinds of questions they might ask the artefact include: what can you tell us about the history of this place; what role do you see yourself performing in our community life; what makes you saddest about our place; what makes you happy; what can you tell us about the culture of the people who made you. These questions can be given to each group as pump primers. Groups should be encouraged to present their dialogue in a creative way—song, poem, play, diary entry, etc. The fun can be extended by the artefacts then having a conversation among themselves. The slide kit can be used as an introduction to this type of activity.

• *Essay competition.* An essay competition can be run using the above concept of a dialogue with some element of the town. The entry form for the competition should be used as an educational device, explaining the concept of how the elements of the town are a reflection of the local culture.

Livability resources and corrosives

What is it that makes living, working and playing in a local area enjoyable? There are tangible community assets— these may be called *livability resources*—that create quality of life. The quantitative assessment of cultural resources will have documented many of these livability resource such as libraries and good restaurants. But many of the things that contribute to the quality of life in a community are not physical commodities that can be simply counted.

For example, some cities and towns feel mean-spirited. Others have a co operative and caring attitude, a bank of goodwill which Chris Cunningham (1994) refers to as the *altruistic surplus:*

> If competition and conflict were really the ruling forces in urban society then our cities would resemble Beirut or Sarajevo. If cities are working even tolerably well then it must be because considerable numbers of citizens are contributing more than they draw out. The trait of

> altruism...is the distinguishing force that keeps the city
> functioning...The obvious signs of a healthy city, where
> there is a strong altruistic surplus, are a strong sense of
> community, a feeling of doing things together, and a caring
> ethos...The greatest threat to the city is the diminution of
> the altruistic surplus of its citizens.

This altruistic surplus can make an enormous difference in the livability of a city. In Portland USA, for example, residents have raised money, with no help from government, to progressively buy pieces of bushland to be preserved as an environmental park. The last block cost $600,000—all of which came from personal donations. A car park, which has been converted into a people's square in the centre of town, was paid for by donations from the community. The high level of citizen involvement in making Portland a better place for future generations is what makes Portland stand out in contrast to many other US cities. Other livability resources that are not easily measured include such things as the creative wealth of an area. Some cities have a spirit of innovation which is infectious. In other cities the creative spark seems to have died, or is burning very low. Creativity needs fuel and a supportive environment. Some areas have more of both.

Areas can also have 'negative commodities' which act as *livability corrosives*—things like fear of crime—which diminish livability. In developing a culture, these 'anti-culture agents' must be diminished or controlled. Livability resources and corrosives are intimately entwined with culture. Livability resources are both the result of a culture and the facilitator of culture. Corrosives are the result of culture and a negative force in the culture. Cultural development should improve quality of life by targeting the livability resources that need bolstering and reducing the impact of the corrosives.

It is the nature of most livability resources and corrosives that they cannot be measured or quantified directly. However, it is possible to get an *indication* of the health or strength of each resource or corrosive by examining what the resources or corrosives produce. For example, an indication of the health of the altruistic surplus may be the number of hours spent in voluntary community service, or the percentage of income donated to community organisations, or the percentage of the population not maximising their income so they can spend time building relationships or serving the community. In order to make these *indicators* even more useful, they can be converted into *benchmarks* against which progress can be measured.

Even though the whole concept of livability resources and corrosives, and the use of indicators and benchmarks, are still in infancy, they are a powerful tool in helping evolve a cultural development strategy. In fact they can form the entire backbone of a community/cultural/quality-of-life study. The state of Oregon in the USA uses quality-of-life indicators or benchmarks as its major policy framework, using them as a guide to budgeting and evaluation of performance. (For more information on livability resources, indicators and benchmarks, and for a pump-primer list of livability resources and corrosives, see Appendix B.)

Livability or quality-of-life workshop

A workshop can be convened which encourages participants to think holistically about:

- All the factors that contribute to their enjoyment of living, working and playing in their local area, and those elements which distract
- Ways that these resources and corrosives can be measured
- Their perceptions of the strengths and weaknesses of each
- Which resources and corrosives they would like to see changed the most.

The workshop can be run with mixed interest groups, or can be run with separate special interest groups. The added advantage of separate groups is that each workshop session takes on a life and direction of its own and produces different results reflecting the make-up and experiences of the group. These unique insights can be useful in subsequent strategy formulation in making strategies more responsive to different needs within the community.

The starting point for this workshop can be a summary of livability resources and corrosives that have emerged during the previous mapping exercises. In the background or foreground of most contributions to the mapping exercises, there will be a livability resource or corrosive. These can be extracted and listed before the workshop. This list can be supplemented by the list in Appendix B.

The term *livability resource* will be even more foreign to most residents than *culture*. The workshop needs to start with some explanation of the concepts explained in this section. This also means that care needs to be taken in how the workshops are titled. References to lifestyle or quality of life are likely to be more meaningful than an invitation to 'improve your livability resources and diminish your livability corrosives'.

Mapping access and access barriers

It may be important, when forming the cultural development strategy, to identify groups within the community experiencing intellectual, cultural, economic and physical barriers which restrict or prevent access to cultural resources and activities. It would also be handy to have some clues as to how these barriers may be removed.

Groups likely to be experiencing access problems due to language barriers, cultural mores, economic pressures, or a combination of these factors, will typically include non-English-speaking-background groups, particularly the women from those communities, and Aboriginal and Torres Strait Islander groups. Low income households (particularly female-headed, single-parent households with dependent children) people with disabilities, older people, young people and the unemployed will all have their particular access problems. Some indications of which groups you will need to talk to should emerge from the demographic profiles and also from the cultural group mappings. Each of these groups should have an opportunity to contribute at this stage—but on their 'turf', at their time, and at their pace. These groups can be asked how they would like to portray the barriers they experience.

Charting coordination opportunities

In the strategy stage it will be important to identify opportunities for coordination of efforts and aspirations in order to better utilise scarce resources. The specific objectives of this mapping are to:

- Identify other groups within the community which may be undertaking strategic planning exercises and examine the potential for joint activities in both the planning and implementation stages

They had to hold the council meeting under a tree in the carpark. Overnight Cr Morton had become a paraplegic and Cr 'Franky' Abbotsford had become a single parent with another on the way.

- Identify external bodies with interests in coordinating activities in specific areas (artform peak bodies; ethnic, community, Aboriginal and Torres Strait Islander organisations; council, etc.) and determine how your community can maximise the benefits from cooperation with these bodies
- Review the potential for sub-regional or regional cooperation with communities in other local government areas to determine the potential for specialisation, economies of scale and individual identity or cultural differentiation.

This mapping could be done in an invitation workshop involving the appropriate agencies, government officers and community representatives. Relevant information should be extracted from the study and circulated as background material. This stage will provide opportunities for forming strategic alliances with groups with similar or complementary objectives, thus increasing the critical mass of people working towards cultural development. These potential alliances or areas of cooperation will be part of the input data for the SWOT (strengths, weaknesses, opportunities, threats) workshop (detailed in Chapter 5) which starts the stragegy-formation phase. It should also provide opportunities for cross-fertilisation of ideas in preparation for the future visions workshop in the following planning stage. The primary aim of this workshop is to explore the *potential* for alliances and cooperation rather than forming those alliances. Such actions will come after the visioning and strategy planning phases.

Self-perception questionnaire/workshop

All of the above qualitative exercises have been aimed at helping organisers and participants get a feeling for how the community views itself, what are the current levels of satisfaction with the living environment, and clues as to what may need to change. One way of testing these issues is to conduct a qualitative survey.

The survey does not need to be statistically based, as long as you are happy that you are gathering a sufficiently diverse range of views and experiences. You can divide it up into parts, each targeted at different groups, such as:

- The public
- Political, community and business leaders
- Various experts in different fields, such as key artsworkers, arts or cultural administrators, academics, etc.
- Different community groupings such as ethnic groups, older people, young people, teachers, media representatives etc.

The survey can ask open-ended questions like:

- What do you think of as the main feature of the cultural life of our community?
- What represents the best of our community's culture? Why?
- What represents the worst of our community's culture? Why?
- What sort of reputation do you think our community's cultural offerings have within the overall life of the shire/town? Within the region? Among visitors?
- Is that reputation deserved? What can be done to make it better or more distinctively ours?
- What would you say are our most important needs for cultural development?

These questions assume that the respondents understand what you mean by 'culture'. If they don't, some explanation needs to be given. Alternatively, the wording should be changed to something like, 'If you were a tourist visiting our city, what do you think would strike you most about our culture—our way of life, the personality of our city?'

An alternative would be to conduct a survey at the end of the mapping exercises as a means of further testing the outcomes. It can ask people to indicate the degree to which they support or disagree with opinions offered during the process; for example, 'To what degree do you agree with the following statement: 'Our town tends to feel inferior to...'.

Another approach to collecting the same information is to hold one or a series of self-perception workshops. The process is exactly the same, except instead of interviewing the target respondents individually, you invite them along to the workshop/s and lead them through the same questioning process.

Using workshops

The cultural planning process is designed to enable meaningful community participation in all aspects of assessment and planning. Although, for practical reasons, it is necessary that the final product be documented by a small team under the editorial control of the project manager and guidance of the steering committee, ample opportunity for community input should be available throughout. The most common method of input is through workshops. Already several have been suggested in the assessment stage and more will be suggested for the strategy development and implementation stage.

The workshops and meetings may be best spread across several months. You may find that your steering committee wishes to combine and collapse several workshops into an intensive period. This decision can only be made with reference to local circumstances and the rate of progress with which your local community feels most comfortable. Consideration should be given to running the same workshop a number of times in different locations if:

- Large populations exceed the comfortable limits for one workshop
- Not all people can attend on the chosen date
- The area is too large or diverse to allow full participation.

Attendance

Workshops seem to work best when there are sufficient attendees to represent a wide range of experiences and opinions. This usually equates with a lower limit of 20 or 30. Upper limits are generally dictated by accommodation constraints. The methodologies in this handbook are sufficiently robust to cope with crowds of several hundred, providing there are enough facilitators to assist.

Workshops should ideally attract a minimum audience of about 50 people, regardless of the size of the community. If you have fewer people than this, there is a danger of the output being too narrowly based to be considered 'representative'. Attendances between 50 and 100 typically gives the best combination of critical mass, energy and comfort. A wide spectrum of attendees will also generally result in lots of good ideas and suggestions being generated.

If the first public workshop in the cultural development strategy process is not well supported, either in terms of low numbers or if there are large sections of the community not represented, it may be necessary to do some additional promotion of the process before starting on the next stage. If preliminary feedback indicates there is likely to be more than 300 attendees, it may be necessary to hold more than one workshop.

As part of the preparation for the workshops, the project team should use the stakeholder list already generated to ensure that relevant stakeholders are notified and invited. Busy people usually need four to six weeks' notice. The general public needs a reminder about the workshop a couple of days beforehand. These personal approaches should be supplemented by:

- Brochures or invitations in arts or cultural organisations' mail-outs
- Press releases
- Notice of meeting advertisements in press and on local radio
- Posters and leaflets
- Telephone ring-around by steering committee members and office bearers of relevant organisations.

Venue and facilities

Running the workshops requires a large meeting space with walls where sheets of butchers paper can be displayed. A screen or white wall for overhead transparencies, slide projector, computer screenshow or video screening may also be necessary. This space should comfortably seat the entire audience, including facilitators (up to 200 in large population areas). This space is where you do your large-group work. The local shire hall or high school auditorium is an ideal venue for a large group.

Schools are particularly good venues because you usually need space for small group work. Small groups ideally number ten participants and each small group needs a space of its own where it can discuss issues and make creative contributions. Each small group will need wall space for butchers paper and an informal seating arrangement around a working area. Tea, coffee and biscuits are normally provided, with a sandwich lunch for day-long workshops.

Scheduling the workshops

To encourage participants to attend all the workshops, it is suggested that a schedule of dates and venues be published four to six weeks before the date of the first workshop so that at the outset all participants are more aware of the commitment they will be making. Consideration should be given to running the most important workshops a number of times in various locations.

Presenters and facilitators

Each workshop will require a presenter who controls the agenda and facilitates the large-group sessions. This person should be conversant with the overall cultural planning process and be comfortable with communicating in a relaxed and positive manner with large numbers of people. Presenters do not necessarily have to be familiar with the particular cultural issues of your area, as the role is that of a facilitator, not an expert. However a broad understanding of cultural matters is an advantage.

Small groups can self-facilitate depending on the complexity of the task. If groups are self-facilitated, it is a good idea to produce a set of guidelines, breaking the small-group process down into a series of simple steps and giving guidance on how long they should spend on each step. The advantage of self-facilitation is that the groups tend to have a greater sense of ownership of the outcomes. The disadvantage is that there is a greater possibility of the groups being dominated by one individual or the group not sticking to their task. This potential problem can be mitigated by having a number of roving facilitators who can quickly recognise if a group is in trouble. Alternatively, a number of 'roving experts' can be made available as a resource for the groups to use as the need arises.

If you are using facilitators, you will need to identify at least one facilitator for every 10 people expected to attend. Good facilitators do not 'lead' the small groups but rather assist them to follow the workshop outline and to arrive at the desired outcome. A handbook on group facilitation, produced in-house by the Queensland Department of Business Industry and Regional Development (DBIRD, 1993), lists the following attributes for the process of facilitation:

- Designing an appropriate process to achieve the outcome desired by the group
- Observing what is happening or not happening in the group and highlighting this to the group
- Identifying and raising problems that are holding the group back
- Drawing out ideas
- Posing new approaches for problem solving.

Appendix A sets out in greater detail a number of the qualities and procedures involved in good facilitation.

Output

Workshops represent a major commitment in time and resources, both from the organisers and attendees. The results are valuable and should be carefully recorded and fully analysed and interpreted. The ongoing participation of attendees is also vital to the process. Attendees should therefore receive a 'thank you' note and a summary of the findings. Although this is a time-consuming and costly exercise, it is necessary to ensure their continuing support, interest and participation.

Group processes

Appendix A contains detailed instructions for running small and large group sessions. A number of texts and references on group processes are listed in the bibliography. Besides the traditional workshop, these texts explain how to run:

- Search conferences organised around a single theme or objective and with a trained facilitator
- Smaller focus group meetings with targeted groups of key stakeholders and a facilitator
- Vision workshops and brainstorming sessions to determine objectives and the way they fit together in a comprehensive plan.

They also contain useful hints. For example, one method of helping groups order their thinking is the 'yellow sticky' method. This technique involves participants writing down their input on yellow self-adhesive notelet squares and sticking them onto butchers paper. The yellow stickies can then be rearranged and/or the results written up in appropriate order on butchers paper or OHP transparencies.

A voting system using stick-on coloured dots can be used for prioritising lists of ideas. Each participant is issued with a set number of the coloured dots (for example, five or ten) and is asked to distribute these according to what they see as the priorities. If you wish to restrict voting for 'pet subjects', participants can be limited to no more than two or three votes (dots) per entry.

Using community artists and imagination

Because most planners and decision makers are most comfortable with didactic and 'logical' ways of processing information, workshops tend to follow the traditional talk-fest pattern. One way of generating ideas for new approaches to running workshops is to talk to some community artists/facilitators about the methods they can suggest for obtaining the same information in a more creative manner. The Community Arts Network is an important resource for putting you in contact with the most appropriate people. This chapter has contained some ideas that can be incorporated into your workshops. The best methodologies will be those designed with your particular audience and your particular needs in mind.

In planning your workshops, it is best to use methods which:

- Allow people to be expansive, but prevent irrelevance
- Allow contributions in random sequence, but produces results with structure and pattern
- Probe for the creative and unexpected, but ensure that basic, anticipated points are all covered.

Documenting and displaying maps

The outcomes from the qualitative assessment of your cultural resources and assets should be documented as an information paper that can be distributed to participants before the next stage, strategy development. This will be a 'sister' information paper to the one produced for the quantitative phase of the assessment and can be incorporated with that paper as background material in your final cultural development strategy document. To increase interest and participation in the next phase of the study, you may consider using the maps generated from this phase as a display.

5 Vision, strategy and implementation

SWOT—taking stock
Establishing the future visions
Developing strategies
Evaluating strategic options
Action Plan
Implementation
Funding the strategy
Managing implementation
Where to from here?

No one had ever noticed it before. But right in the middle of the SWOT workshop, everyone saw it at once—a wart on the council chamber ceiling, right above the Queen. Cr Jones, quoting from The Cultural Planning Handbook, *suggested they transform the weakness into a strength.*

5 Vision, Strategy & Implementation

Armed with a much clearer understanding of the quantity and quality of your cultural resources, the next stage is to evolve your cultural development strategy. Building on the assessment process, this chapter details a series of workshops to take your community through four distinct steps. The first is to take stock of what you have uncovered during the assessment stage and to make a sober judgement as to your current reality, warts and all. The second is to establish a vision of where you want to be at some point in the future. The third is to decide what strategies and actions you are going to use to reach your imagined future. The fourth is to evolve an action plan—and implement it! All stakeholders should be encouraged to participate in this strategy formation, even if they were not involved in the assessment process.

SWOT—taking stock

The assessment process will have uncovered a huge amount of information, which you would now have available in your information papers. One way of systematically drawing this together and using it as input into the visioning and strategising processes is to undertake a SWOT analysis—a stocktake of strengths, weaknesses,

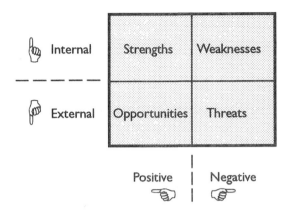

Fig. 5.1 SWOT analysis, a systematic approach

opportunities and threats. SWOT is a powerful tool for examining issues in a strategic framework (figure 5.1). Strengths and weaknesses relate to the *internal* qualities of the community and its organisations, whereas opportunities and threats are *external* circumstances and forces acting on the community and its organisations.

Naming the strengths and weaknesses is important not only for working out *what* you want, but also *how* you are going to get it. Strategies have to be devised that trade on strengths and compensate for the weaknesses. Undertaken by a council, A SWOT analysis may answer the following questions about the council's internal strengths and weakness:

- What is the current level of knowledge regarding cultural issues?
- What is the level of commitment to cultural development?
- What staff and resources are dedicated to cultural issues?
- What influence do staff responsible for cultural development have within the decision-making process?
- To what extent is there participation on regional or state level peak bodies or forums?
- What access do we have to cultural training programs?

The analysis of opportunities and threats (the external forces acting on the council) may answer questions like:

- What changing demands are being made by state and federal governments on councils to provide and coordinate cultural services?
- What development pressures will be placed on council by external tourism operators and how may this impact on local culture?
- How will demographic changes, such as the aging population, impact on the demands for culture-related services?
- How will changing world economies effect the local and regional economy and what impact may this have on the local culture?

It should also be noted that the same phenomenon can be both a threat and an opportunity. When considering threats, it is therefore imperative that that the question be answered, 'What opportunities are presented by this threat?'

When considering strengths, weaknesses, opportunities and threats, most attention is usually given to the strengths and opportunities. This is where most people feel comfortable. It's positive, proactive and uncomplicated. On the other hand, weaknesses and threats cause feelings of discomfort. They seem negative, reactive and complicate the picture. They seemingly diminish the viability of good ideas. But visions and strategies that do not consider weakness and threats are built on a faulty foundation that will ultimately fail. A cultural development strategy must include strategies to overcome weaknesses and transform threats into opportunities. Weakness and threat strategies require more thought and they are harder work.

SWOT workshop

It is recommended that the SWOT analysis be undertaken as a workshop. A suggested agenda is:

- Welcome and opening address
- Format and objectives of workshop
- Small group session —
  - What are the strengths and weaknesses of our local culture?

- – What are the strengths and weaknesses of the local organisa-
  tions which have some impact on our culture?
- – What are the strengths and weaknesses of the council?
- – What are the opportunities for cultural development, and what
  threats must we guard against?
- Large-group session summarising small group findings and vot-
  ing on priorities
- Closure and thanks.

The above agenda would be extremely hard to work through in a
two-and-a-half-hour evening workshop. Ways of making this workshop more time efficient are:

- Have someone extract preliminary answers to the four questions
  from the community input at the assessment stage. The questions
  then become, 'Which strengths and weakness of our local culture
  have we missed, and which do you disagree with?' etc. This avoids
  reinventing the wheel.
- Start group one on question 1, group two on question 2, etc. (Group
  five starts on question 1, group six on question 6.) Each small group
  is asked to examine their starting question in-depth then move
  onto the next question. The advantage of this approach is that you
  get a more in-depth analysis of each of the questions than if every
  group is asked to examine every question more superficially.
- This workshop can be held first with council officers and the results presented to the community for addition and refinement. In
  any case, it is advisable to get the council to look at its own strengths
  and weaknesses before the community is asked to do so.
- The workshop can be held as a half-day workshop, or combined
  with the future visions workshop to form a whole-day workshop.

The small-group session can be divided into two sessions with two
questions addressed in each session. The yellow sticky method can
be employed in all sessions, especially if groups are asked to arrange
their contributions in order of importance. The yellow stickies are

also useful in creating a master-list. As each group reports back, the facilitator takes the yellow sticky and puts it on the master-list. This means the master-list can also be reorganised according to input from the other groups. If some form of voting on importance is required, then it is best to do this after the reporting session so that everyone is voting on the same list. The small groups may be re-convened and the coloured-dot method used for voting. Alternatively the voting can be done in the large group through a simple showing of hands and recording the score for each. If weighting is required, people can be given five votes and can raise two hands if they want to spend two of their votes on the one item.

One useful device for thinking about opportunities and threats is to organise input under three headings of supply, demand and facilitation. A key question can be asked for each:

- *Supply:* what have we got a lot of, or are specially good at?
- *Demand:* what do people want that they can't currently get?
- *Facilitation:* what can we do to get people and ideas together?

Establishing the future visions

The objectives of this stage are to:
- Get participants to think creatively about the future cultural environment of their area
- Obtain a balanced perspective on what type of community participants would like to have in the future.

Future visions workshop

One traditional method is a future visions workshop, designed as a two-and-a-half-hour evening session. A typical agenda could be:
- Welcome and opening address
- Format and objectives of workshop
- Orientation speech

- Large-group session
  - What issues and trends are likely to impact on our local culture?
- Small-groups session
  - What are the main topic areas we need to deal with in constructing our preferred future vision?
  - How do we want our community to be in twenty years?
- Large group session summarising small group findings. Voting
- Closure and thanks.

The large group session on issues and trends is aimed at getting people to think in the following strategic terms:

- 10 to 20 years ahead
- The inevitability of change
- Connections between culture, economics, social conditions and the environment
- Quality of life
- Economic and employment implications.

The first small group question—*What are the main topic areas we need to deal with...?*—starts people thinking in very general terms about the main features of the type of place they would like to live in. These become the headings by which that ideal future place could be described and would generally feature words like: environment, transport, shopping, health, education, beaches, employment, happiness, communication, technology, and culture. These headings can be derived by facilitators asking people to call out suggestions, writing them up and sorting them into groups.

The second small group question regarding the shape of the community in twenty years is ideally suited to the yellow sticky method. The facilitator writes up on butchers paper all the headings the group has come up with, then each participant spends 10 minutes writing down their ideas as key words or sentences, then places them on the butchers paper next to the appropriate heading. The facilitator and group should ask questions of clarification after each contribution. After all suggestions are made, the participants can spend ten minutes sorting the ideas, and if necessary, reworking the wording. Participants can then vote on which they think are the ten most important. Vision elements that are not within the top ten are recorded for possible future reference, but do not go on the list which goes to the large group for voting. A typical top-ten list from a group may be:

- Culture—maintain rural town friendliness—27 [votes]
- Social—services for youth and older people will be improved—26
- Jobs—local people given preference in new projects in shire—24
- Culture—continue subsidies for art prize and drama festival—22
- Environment—retain and restore vegetation along creeks—22
- Tourism—eco/cultural tours to hinterland provide new jobs—20
- Culture—access to arts training for intending professionals—18
- Transport—reduce dependence on cars for local transport—17
- Indigenous residents—local Aboriginal groups become valued part of community life—17
- Economy—greater diversity, reduce unemployment—16

The final large group session should be used to combine the inputs from all small groups into an integrated community future vision statement. A representative of each small group should present their list to the large group. Lists are compared to eliminate duplication, then the large group votes to prioritise the resultant list. The final results of the workshop may then be documented and studied by the steering committee and project team for re-working into a set of cultural development goals and objectives.

'Three wishes' format

An alternative workshop format uses the following technique. Every person at the workshop is given three pieces of paper or card as they enter the workshop. While still in the large group, they are told that for five minutes they can play fairy god-mother. They have three wishes and they can change anything about their community and its cultural life they want. They are encouraged to write one wish on each of the cards. They then break into small groups to share their wishes. The group then refines these wishes into vision statements and choose their top ten. The rest of the workshop follows the same format as above.

The advantage with this approach is that, for a brief moment, it places people in a world of make-believe where there are no limits and all things are possible. It is only in this frame of mind that creative ideas are born. Unless people have a natural ability to enter this

Cr Jones thought it was just an old miners lanten—a cultural relic of the past. But out of the blue, right in the middle of the future visions workshop, the old genie miner connected past, present and future.

realm of play, they may find it hard to think creatively and will unconsciously censor their own ideas by saying 'But that's crazy'. Often in small-group work, someone will say something which is totally 'off the wall'. The rest of the group agrees that it is crazy, but one person will respond, 'Well maybe it's not such a crazy idea. We may not be able to do X, but surely we could do Y.' Lateral thinking is the process of derailing normal thinking processes and putting them unexpectedly on a new track. Techniques, such as the three wishes or the role-play below, aid the creative process.

Role play format

Before the workshop, a number of 'typical' characters are created which represent some of the divergent cultural groups in the community. For example there may be: Slasher, a 45-year-old cane farmer; Amanda, a 28-year-old quadriplegic; Jason, a seven-year-old; B.J. the property developer; Crystal, a 50-year-old artist who works as a volunteer at the Environment Centre; Malcolm, a 75-year-old-retiree; and Launa, a single mum with two pre-school children. The audience is divided into the number of characters you have created. The easiest way to do this is: if there are ten characters, number people from 1 to 10 with all the ones being in group 1, all the twos in group 2, etc. (This approach has the added advantage of splitting up interest blocks.) Groups should have no more than eight people, so it pays to have more characters prepared than you think you will actually need. Each group is given a character and asked to describe the perfect living environment for its character if they were living in your city/town in twenty years' time.

They are then instructed to imagine that they have been transported back in time to a public meeting where your city/town is deciding its vision for the future. The small group, still in their assigned characters, have to construct a list of ten vision statements which they will take to this public meeting to ensure that their perfect future comes to pass. When the large group reconvenes, each group presents its version of the ideal community and cultural environment together with their vision statements. The role-play can be continued with all groups staying in role while asking questions of clarification and discussing the ideas put up by other groups. To facilitate this, the character names can be printed on a placard and each group remains around their placard. The facilitator should encourage groups to address each other in role.

The lists are then combined as for the first workshop. It is recommended that during this process, and for the final voting, people come out of role. This is necessary to anchor the vision in reality, even though it has been conceived in play.

One advantage of this process is that it aids creative thinking as did the 'three wishes' process. An additional advantage is that it helps people think much more holistically and helps get them off their pet hobby-horses. Workshop attendees are usually from a limited range of cultural groupings in the community. Or to put it another way, there is usually a wide range of cultural groupings either under-represented or totally missing from most workshops. This may be in spite of the organisers' best efforts. The role play technique helps people to think inclusively and to 'get inside other people's skins'. The vision statements that emerge from this process are likely to be much more inclusive and equitable.

Check for compatibility

The output of the future vision workshop is a statement by the attendees, as representatives of a wide cross-section of the community, as to what sort of society, economy, environment or place they would like to live in 20 years' time. This should be checked for compatibility with any similar statements from such sources as:

- The land-use strategy or town plan
- Council's corporate plan
- Any other strategy plans for the area, such as transport, economic development, human services or tourism strategies.

Those councils which already have policy statements may choose to start here, but it would not be recommended unless the policy statements have been based on the type of rigorous research and consultation process outlined above.

Draft Mission Statement

When the working party has documented the future vision workshop output into a balanced statement of what sort of future the community wants, this should be converted into a more structured format of mission statement, goals and objectives. A mission statement should summarise, in a relatively short statement, the core focus and the scope of your vision. This draft mission statement can be broad and strategic, for example:

> To formulate a cultural development strategy for Utopia Shire which will foster appreciation of and involvement in the diverse cultural resources and activities of the area and to develop programs in heritage, the arts, cultural tourism and indigenous cultures which will enhance quality of life for shire residents and make it an attractive place to visit.

Or, it could be a more targeted mission statement such as:

> To develop a strategy and programs which will assist the young people of the area in gaining access to skills in design, fashion and media production.

Whichever type of mission statement you choose, you will need to follow this up by outlining a series of goals and objectives which will enable you to achieve this vision.

Draft Goals and Objectives

Goals and objectives are, moving down from the broad vision through the mission statement, more tangible, specific statements of how the vision will be achieved. Your goals and objectives will, of course, be determined by local conditions and options. In the next stage of the cultural development process, these goals and objectives will be converted into an action plan—the nuts and bolts of how the goals and objectives will be realised. It is important that this process of converting the vision into goals and objectives be completed thoroughly and reviewed by the steering committee, as they will be used later in the process to evaluate alternative strategy options. This list of goals and objectives should be treated as a draft until it has been tested in some form of community consultation—either as a draft paper made available for comment or as the first stage of a strategy brainstorm workshop.

Information review

To prepare for the strategy making process, and in order to be as focused and informed as possible, it may be a good idea to pause slightly and review all the information you have in the light of the recently decided goals and objectives. The cultural development planning process may have been going now for up to twelve months. Some of the good ideas and information that surfaced early in the process may have slipped off the agenda. Now is a good chance to conduct a review to get things into a wider perspective.

As you read each document, or review original meeting notes, ask yourself what the significance of each item is. New connections will suggest themselves. Note these down. It is useful to adopt an audit

trail for significant comments, to keep track of them and tie them into strategies or projects later in the process. If this point in the process is being used for a final edit on the material produced to date, the project manager should get the steering committee to go over the documentation carefully to make sure that it reads well from the perspective of somebody who is not fully conversant with the subject matter.

Developing strategies

The next stage requires the completion of several tasks, some of which can be tackled in tandem, within the one activity:

- Agreement on mission statement, goals and objectives
- Brainstorming potential pathways (strategies) which will result in realisation of the vision spelt out in the goals and objectives
- Evaluating the potential strategies and choosing those which are implementable within the constraints of current reality
- Turning the strategies into action plans—deciding who will do what, when.

Strategy brainstorming workshop

The next step is to convene a workshop to generate ideas for the strategy. These ideas should build on the information assembled to date. It is suggested that participation in this workshop be limited to people who have attended one or more of the previous workshops and that each participant be sent a briefing document including the background information, SWOT analysis, results of the vision workshop and the draft mission statement, goals and objectives. A suggested agenda for a half-day workshop is:

- Welcome and opening address
- Format and objectives of workshop
- Questions of clarification re: draft mission statement, goals and objectives

- Small groups: question—*What changes or additions would we like to see to the draft mission statement, goals and objectives?*
- Large group: report back and testing of consensus on suggested changes
- Small groups: question—*What course of actions could lead us to reaching our goals and objectives?*
- Large group: report back and voting on actions
- Closure and thanks.

In the large-group session, the ideas from each small group are pooled and voted on, as in the SWOT workshop. This gives a good indication of the direction in which the community would like to move, but the output at this stage will need considerable reworking and structuring to get it into the format of a draft strategy.

Role play alternative

It is important for participants to think creatively about how they are going to get to their imagined future. If the role-play technique was used in helping to establish the future vision, it can be used again to evolve strategies. The same character groups are reformed. They are reminded of the vision that their characters evolved in the previous workshop. They are then asked to invent a story which shows how the community moved from where it is now to the future they imagined. After telling their story to the larger group, other groups (preferably still in role) ask questions about the story. These questions are usually along the lines 'Yes, but how were the council officers convinced to spend this extra money on...?' It is these questions that start to force the construction of more realistic scenarios. Small groups can then reconvene and make lists of potential actions and strategies. Alternatively, this could be moderated in the larger group, depending on the size of the audience.

Consideration should be given to combining the *strategy* workshop with the *future visions* workshop, making a half- to full-day workshop. This means that the visions do not have to be restated and people can simply stay in character. The disadvantage is that the steering committee will not have time to convert the outcomes from the visioning exercise into goals and objectives or to carry out the information review. This problem can be avoided if the goals and objectives are extracted after the initial strategy brainstorm. It should be remembered that the reason for producing goals and objectives from the vision is to use them in *selecting the best strategies* and as a means of measuring performance in the implementation stage. They are not necessarily essential to generating potential strategies if the overall vision is clearly articulated.

Creating a checklist or organising framework

Organisers may find it useful to have an 'organising framework' that can act as a means of refining and organising ideas and to be a checklist after the brainstorming. One approach is to create a matrix. (See figure 5.2.) The X-axis of the matrix divides the study area into a number of geographical districts within which specific strategies are to be considered. Although each area is different, for practical purposes it is suggested that you use no more than six districts. The final column on the X-axis deals with strategy ideas that cover the entire study area. Other columns can be added, depending on the nature of the strategy. For example, a column may be added for the council organisation. The Y-axis of the matrix contains the issues or strategy areas to be addressed.

This matrix approach is flexible. For example, instead of geographical areas on the X axis, you may choose to list the cultural groupings that were identified in the cultural groups mapping exercise. The Y-axis may be the goals and objectives. Alternatively, you may choose to construct a number of matrices.

If the matrix idea is introduced too early into the workshop, there is a danger that people will become overly preoccupied with constructing this 'scaffolding' rather than the building inside the scaffolding. It is therefore suggested that either this concept is not intro-

Strategy areas	District 1	District 2	District 3	Whole shire
Visual & performing arts				
Contemporary arts				
Heritage				
Cultural tourism				

Fig. 5.2 Matrix to be used as organising framework and checklist

duced till later in the process or that groups be encouraged only to change the organising framework in response to what they discover as they brainstorm the strategies. In other words, deficiencies in the organising framework will become evident as they construct their strategy.

Building the strategy

Many of the ideas from the workshops will be partial measures which need fleshing out or combining with other ideas in order to evolve a coherent strategy. For example, the workshop may have identified promoting drama workshops, professional productions and an annual puppet festival in District 3 as major initiatives. When the project group looks at the logistics and potential of other suggestions, it might find that this suggestion can be expanded by: placing it within a larger excellence-in-performing-arts 'envelope', involving Districts 1 and 6 and the two Shires to the north and west; and supporting the initiative through ongoing promotional and training programs and the strategic linkage of projects, programs and personnel.

The project team now has to pull all the inputs from the process to date into a strategic framework. This may vary from area to area, according to local needs and preferences, but each strand of an integrated local area strategic planning system could consist of the following elements:

- Dynamic *database* to inform the strategy and, later, to provide some performance indicators
- *Vision* or *mission statement* and set of *goals and objectives* to give direction and quality standards
- Enabling *programs* which support and facilitate cultural development—maintaining a database, market research, networking, newsletters, fund-raising, training, lobbying etc.
- *Projects* which are discrete jobs that the council (or strategy manager designated by the council) chooses to undertake to achieve a particular strategic objective
- *Linkages* which are projects that may occur under other strategies, but which have cultural implications.

Linkages may be an appropriate way of dealing with some issues that have cultural implications but are essentially matters that are being handled by others under a different strategy. An example of this may be a proposal to reuse an historic building as a tourist attraction. Although this has cultural significance, the matter may be dealt with by the council's tourism or economic development group. The linkage back to its cultural significance may be dealt with by having a 'cultural' person sitting on the project committee or by obliging the proponents of the tourism project to consult with a cultural standing committee on heritage sites, which may have been established for that purpose.

The first draft of the strategy should include an audit of the comments and findings from earlier research and workshops to ensure that all information and opinions have been given due consideration.

Evaluating strategic options

A summary of the projects/programs should be produced and a list of possible viable alternatives should be matched against each. These programs and projects and the alternatives should then be documented for distribution before the strategy evaluation workshop or for presentation at the workshop. If it is to be presented at the workshop, the documentation needs to be in a format that enables participants to review each project/program and its associated alternative individually; for example, they may be summarised on butchers paper.

The final workshop has been designed to enable participants to review the draft strategy proposal put together by the project team. This involves selecting alternatives, assigning priorities and generally fine-tuning the draft. The framework recommended for this is a technique known as *goals achievement matrix*. A simple example is shown in figure 5.3. This technique provides an open, objective means of assessing the relative merit of different options according to the degree to which they assist in, or detract from, the achievement of the objectives you defined at the start of the process. In the example shown in figure 5.3, a simple scoring system is used where scores are allotted between +3 and -3 depending on how strongly the option contributes towards achieving the goal or objective. Plus values are assigned for a positive contribution, zero for neutral contributions and negative values if they detract. Using the example in figure 5.3, option F is the best overall, with a score of ten. This simple system treats all objectives as being of equal value; that is, no weightings have been applied.

A slightly more complex system uses simple weighting by distributing 100 *brownie points* between the various objectives. If a particular objective receives 16 brownie points, then each option for achieving this objective is given a score out of 16 for how well that option fulfils that particular objective. An example of how to use this system

Objective	A	B	C	D	E	F
Quality	0	+1	+2	-3	0	+2
Creative development	+2	0	-1	-1	+1	+2
Lifestyle	-1	+1	-1	+2	0	+1
Business assistance	-1	-2	0	0	+1	+3
Networking	+3	+2	+1	+3	+1	-1
Cultural diversity	+1	+3	-1	+2	+1	+3
Regional identity	0	+1	+1	+2	+3	0
Total	**+5**	**+6**	**+1**	**+5**	**+7**	**+10**

Figure 5.3 Goals achievement matrix

Objective	Brownie Points	A	B	C	D	E	F
Quality	10	5	7	9	1	5	8
Creative development	20	17	10	7	8	13	16
Lifestyle	16	8	9	5	15	9	10
Business assistance	8	3	2	4	5	5	8
Networking	15	15	13	11	14	10	7
Cultural diversity	17	8	16	7	15	13	17
Regional identity	14	7	8	9	12	14	7
Total	**100**	**53**	**65**	**52**	**70**	**70**	**73**

Figure 5.4 Weighted goals achievement matrix

is shown in figure 5.4. Under this assessment system, option F still comes out best. This system gives a clearer indication of which options give the best fit while considering the relative importance of each objective.

These assessment processes have one drawback: they can overlook the strategic linkages between the options for various objectives.

In other words, an option may have spin-off benefits for another objective, or combine well with another option, producing a multiplier effect. This drawback can be overcome by weighting those options which strategically link with other options. In the final analysis it is human beings, not some evaluation framework, which must make the decision as to the best combination of programs and projects and the best combination of options.

Community input into the final evaluation of strategic options can also be handled in a number of other ways:

• Street corner meetings can be convened where the strategic options are outlined and people are encouraged to ask questions of clarification. They can be asked to vote on options by raising their hands or by filling out a voting sheet. Street corner meetings can encourage wider participation.

• A shop front can be established with a display mapping options and staffed to answer questions. Attendees can be encouraged to fill out a voting sheet.

• Quantitative surveys can be conducted to find out to what extent there is support for various measures. The disadvantage with this is that many people surveyed will not understand the context and will vote out of ignorance thus diluting thoughtful comment by those who do understand the issues.

• Hold focus groups with stakeholders and cultural groups, particularly those to be targeted in improving equity in access to cultural resources. Chances are that the most disadvantaged groups in the community will be under-represented or absent from the workshop. The format of the focus groups can be targeted to the needs of each group. The focus group activity can also take place within existing meeting structures for that group—for example, a social geography class at the high school, the monthly senior citizens' meeting, the Indo-Chinese Social Club meeting, or a meeting for mothers under a tree at the local pre-school immediately following normal drop-off time.

Final adjustments

Following the evaluation, the project team will have to bring the results together into logical, consistent and complementary projects and programs. This may mean they have to add things or move things around in order to get the strategy to balance and work properly.

As emphasised earlier, the cultural development strategy must be integrated with other strategic plans. At the final documentation stage, the cultural development strategy needs to be cross-referenced with other existing or draft strategies for :

- Compatibility of goals and objectives
- Scope of issues (overlaps and service gaps)
- Data collection and analysis requirements
- Implementation plans (for timing conflicts, possible economies of scale in resource utilisation and establishment of linkages).

If the goals and objectives of the cultural development strategy are incompatible with the goals and objectives of the other strategies, you do not necessarily have to change to fit in with them, but it does indicate a need to hold discussions with the other parties to see whether there is, in fact, a problem and what, if anything, can be done about it.

If the compatibility check indicates that you have a lot in common with the goals and objectives of another strategy, you should investigate the potential for mutually supportive actions, joint efforts or resource sharing. This will increase integration and reduce overall costs. This may be developed within the context of Integrated Local Area Planning (ILAP).

Action plan

The resultant projects and programs must then be converted into an *action plan*. Each program and project should be specified in the following terms:

- *Objectives*—what is to be achieved by this program/project
- *Implementation plan*—what steps are involved in carrying it out
- *Responsibility*—who will manage the program/project
- *Budget*—what resources will be required, including a cash flow estimate for the current financial period
- *Timetable*—when the project will be completed (programs are ongoing) and the major milestones by which progress in programs and projects can be judged.

The final draft product should be then reviewed in conjunction with a number of different groups, prior to being submitted to the council for ratification. Reviewers should include:

- Steering committee, for a last check on content and prioritisation of action plans for budgetary purposes
- Designated project managers to ensure that they are still agreeable to managing the nominated projects within the agreed scope, timeframe and budget
- Council administrative executive, to review the compatibility of the strategy with the corporate plan and decision making structure.

Budget

Budgeting for the implementation of the strategy is a major step. By definition, there will always be more things that you want to do than money available. The budgeting will probably take several rounds of pruning and creative thinking about fundraising and hard-headed prioritisation. Due to staggered closing dates for applications for program funding, it may not be possible to accurately forecast income.

The budget should have the following components:

- *Overheads*—includes wages, rent, insurance etc. for larger organisations, and phone, postage, printing, stationery etc. for smaller ones
- *Programs*—the essential activities and services undertaken by all organisations

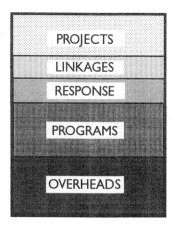

Figure 5.5 Budget elements showing increasing degree of discretion

- *Response*—spare resources which can be used for projects that cannot be foreseen at the start of the budget, such as responding to emergencies, threats or new opportunity
- *Linkages*—the multi-disciplinary projects on which you may wish to be represented
- *Projects*—the major discretionary elements of the strategy which are designed to achieve specific strategic milestones.

Figure 5.5 shows how these elements vary in the degree of discretion involved—from the non-discretionary items you are obliged to do as a consequence of opening the doors, to the discretionary items. Care needs to be taken in ensuring these elements do not grow out of proportion to each other. For example, if half of the budget were spent on overheads, the organisation implementing the strategy may be too top heavy. However, if the budget were heavily skewed in favour of discretionary elements, the implementing body may not be able to function in a proper and sustainable manner.

Prior to developing your strategy, you may have conceived your task as one of simply initiating and managing arts projects. If, as the result of this handbook, you have adopted a broader and deeper perspective on the work you are undertaking, it will be important to ground your projects within a strong developmental framework. To help in this process, it is important to realise that within the cultural portfolios of local government, much of the budget for overheads is often provided by in-kind support and volunteer input. Consideration should be given to including the value of this in-kind support in the budgets. Outside government departments and agencies often look for indications of community support when deciding on granting funds.

Documentation

The Cultural Development Strategy outcomes need to be documented and made publicly available. This would usually take the form of a written report, but may also include other media such as film/video, or more creative forms such drama, music or dance.

Implementation

The last stage—implementation—is, of course, the most difficult. This is where the hard work of transforming dreams into reality begins.

Management

Under the strategic framework outlined above, each project and program should have a designated project manager. Programs, being ongoing exercises, are normally run in-house, so the project manager is normally a designated staff member. Projects, however, can be managed by any competent and experienced person, including:

- Staff or members of council
- Staff or members of an affiliated cultural organisation (Arts Council branch, ethnic community council etc.)
- Consultant or contractor.

The project manager's role involves responsibility for the allocation and expenditure of resources, achievement of agreed milestones and management of the quality of both the process and the final product. Due to the important nature of this task, the process of accountability should be clearly established.

A realistic timetable must be set for each project, taking into account the tasks to be performed and the resources available. Many projects will not involve full-time staff. Hence the importance of gaining your Council's commitment to the strategy through identification of linkages with other council responsibilities. Economic development, community development and urban planning are all areas where your strategy can and should have significant input.

Projects may need to be framed around part-time availability of volunteers. Providing logistical support to volunteer working parties, wherever possible, will speed up the process of implementation, improve the quality of outcomes and will help minimise burnout—a major problem for processes relying too heavily on a small band of committed volunteers.

Even though individual project managers are looking after particular programs/projects, there is still a need for coordination and review. This may be done by forming a interdepartmental working group, a peak forum (such as a *Cultural Development Committee*) or by formalising the steering committee. Alternatively, the council may have an existing committee which could have its ambit broadened to take on this new role. Project managers should submit progress reports on each project at appropriate intervals.

Integration with other strategies

When refining the cultural development strategy, a compatability check was made with other strategic plans. Based on the belief that in the end all elements of activity at the local government level are connected and intertwined, bridges should continue to be built between the various strategic planning bodies; between the council departments, between elected representatives and council officers, between council and community groups including private enterprise, and between council and state and federal government agencies. It is these linkages, that in the final analysis may effect the greatest cultural change.

Council decision-making processes

At the end of the day, many of the important decisions which will mould local culture will be made by your local council. These decisions can quickly undermine or directly contradict the vision of your cultural development strategy—regardless of the quality of your strategic planning document. *All* decisions in council have cultural and community development implications—particularly the infrastructure, land use and economic decisions made daily. Even the Council's *current* organisational structure, decision-making processes, architecture and symbols may covertly subvert the cultural development strategy.

It is therefore recommended that this issue of the corporate culture of the council, and its impact on the cultural development of the community, be kept firmly on the agenda during implementation. Some councils have undertaken a study along these lines *before* launching into the processes outlined in this handbook. If the issues of council culture have not been included in the strategic plan, it is recommended that this issue be viewed at as part of the implementation process.

There are pros and cons regardless of where this review of council culture is located. If done before the cultural development strategy, it helps prepare the council for more informed participation in the strategy development. If done after, it is easier to see what changes may be demanded in council by the development strategy. Regardless, the review needs to be undertaken with the assistance of senior council administrators and managers. If the review is done before the strategy is formulated, then there will still be a need during the implementation stage to review the workloads of those in council with cultural development duties and their resource needs. Reporting processes should also be reviewed to ensure that due consideration of cultural objectives, values and issues is incorporated into the reporting process. Similarly, the degree of compliance with the cultural strategy should be examined when considering any new application or project.

Funding the strategy

Implementing the strategy will require resources, both in cash and in kind. Although it is not necessarily true that the quality of the outcome is directly related to dollars expended, an implementation plan which is not properly funded will result in either an unsatisfactory product or disgruntled team members or both.

Local councils throughout Australia are generally being asked to take on more and more areas of responsibility on budgets which are not expanding at the same rate. State and federal funding for arts and cultural matters has been growing steadily, albeit from a small base. However, the competition for these funds is very keen. In the long term, the most stable platform for developing and improving local culture may be the local community and its business sector.

The viability of this self-help philosophy may depend on the ability of your local peak forum and its constituent cultural organisations and stakeholders to embrace appropriate fundraising and sponsorship programs. There are numerous examples of cultural and sporting organisations tapping into significant private funding sources. Successful models include the Australian Opera, various Olympic bids, the National Basketball League, some of the museum and art gallery acquisition programs, etc. In all these cases, the organisers created a package of benefits and an image to which private sponsors were happy to contribute financially and with which they desired the name of their firms or products to be associated.

Applying for grants and program funding

Part of the funding for implementing the strategy will come from program funding and grants from state and federal departments/ authorities. These will mainly be related to the arts, but could also include tourism and business development funding if parts of the strategy fall into those sectors. Projects can also be structured to qualify for eligibility in other funding areas such as women's programs, rural/remote locations, Aboriginal and Torres Strait Islander, youth, older people, disabled, export incentives, etc.

As the amount of funds for grants is limited and the number of applications always exceeds the amount available, to be successful, grants or program funding applications need to be:

- For a purpose that is related to the objectives of the funding program
- Carefully planned to meet both the external program guidelines and your own strategic objectives (win-win)
- Contain good research design to establish the needs, identify how the needs will be met and identify how the community and the various participants will benefit from the project.

It is strongly recommend that you do not base your strategy entirely around those areas for which you *may* obtain program funding. It is important to have contingency plans should you fail in your grant applications.

Budget accountability

Projects need to have inbuilt budget accountability which covers the authorisation of expenditure, methods of payment and keeping of receipts. Within the budget, key expenditure amounts should be associated with milestones expressed in terms of the percentage of completion.

Any system of financial administration requires documented procedures and a process of checks and balances that ensure:

- Funds are spent on purchasing the goods or services for which they were approved (i.e., you are not taking funds from one area that has been discussed and agreed upon and spending them on something else)
- The timing of expenditure is in accordance with an agreed cashflow rate that is capable of being financed at any time
- The only people who may incur expenses on behalf of the organisation are people explicitly authorised to do so
- Expenditure is only approved by those authorised persons after they are satisfied that the goods or services meet the order specification (e.g., if a consultant submits a progress account in the middle of a job, the work completed to date must be at the level of the agreed milestone—for example, a draft report).

Monitoring and review

Where public money is being spent, an audit process is required to ensure that everything is properly accounted for. In addition to the straight monetary side, the efficiency and effectiveness of the process and its results need to be continually monitored and assessed to ensure that funds and effort are not being wasted. This monitoring and review mechanism needs to be factored into the overall strategy. The simplest method may be a regular meeting between the overall management group and the project and program managers of each element of the strategy.

Managing implementation

Council- or community-driven

This handbook is designed primarily to assist councils to play an active and constructive role in community cultural development. Although many councils throughout Australia are directly and actively involved, many others may choose to delegate the lead role to a community group or committee. The research and strategy formulation sections above are written generally to accommodate situations that are either conducted in-house by council, or facilitated by a committee, with council providing assistance.

Such committees may also be delegated prime responsibility for the implementation, with appropriate support from the council. In some instances this may be the preferred solution. However, councils are inevitably directly involved in cultural policy by virtue of the decisions they make on land use, access to resources and infrastructure and provision of council services. It is therefore essential that they consciously manage the elements of their operation that impact on culture and they are fully aware of the contribution they can make to cultural development through their existing programs. This unavoidable involvement in cultural development needs to be managed and coordinated with the elements of the cultural development strategy being implemented by the committee. This will require a very clear articulation of responsibilities in order to avoid ambiguity. These responsibilities would normally be indicated in a draft policy framework, which would need to be discussed and approved by council as a formal policy. Some structural changes in council decision-making would also need to be made so that when weighing major decisions, the cultural development strategy is given equal status to the other strategic plans such as the preferred land use strategy or financial management strategy.

The advantage of the council-driven model is that the process is initiated, controlled by and remains within the council. Some find this the most direct and administratively simple way to proceed. It has the advantage of being able to tap directly into council resources and infrastructure, such as staff and funding, mail, telephones, vehicles and secretarial support systems. The conventional approach in small councils is the appointment of one or more officers in a branch or section within a larger department to look after cultural development. These are often included with the library or a community development section. Larger councils may have whole departments relating to community services, which include libraries, art galleries, health and welfare.

The other advantage in locating cultural development within the council has to do with the level of ownership of the process and recognition that council is *already* a key player, if not the key player, in cultural development. This is particularly important if cultural development is to have an impact on areas such as land-use planning and transport.

The disadvantages of this model are the temptation to skimp on meaningful consultation and the establishment of partnerships with key stakeholders. Another potential problem occurs when new councils are voted in that do not have the same level of understanding or commitment as the previous administration. This can be offset to some extent if the cultural development consultation process has been used to generate a vocal and supportive 'client-base' for the product.

The best vehicle for the implementation of the strategy under the community-driven model is for the community organisation to become incorporated, which may be achieved under the Companies Act as a not-for-profit company limited by guarantee or as an incorporated association under the relevant state law. This affords a degree of protection for members of the executive and allows the organisation to hire staff, own property, enter into contracts and do most of the things which Australian companies are legally entitled to do. Incorporation also provides for proper decision making and financial management procedures, as well as limiting the legal liability of individual members.

Regional cooperation

To cope with the ongoing scarcity of resources for cultural development, innovative and creative responses are going to be required to make funding and developmental effort stretch further. Particularly in non-metropolitan areas of Australia, one of the best ways of achieving this is through regional cooperation. This requires councils and communities to get together to talk about ways of combining their resources, buying power and activities, sharing facilities and arranging regional tours, etc.

This cooperation can be on an informal basis or on more formal arrangements covering the various forms of joint planning, promotion, development and action. These arrangements can be in the form of artform or issue specific networks or geographical groupings or as working parties that are formed for specific projects and which are disbanded when the objectives are achieved.

Fifteen years ealier Cr Jones had sent the mayor in the adjoining shire a particularly ugly potato-man, remarking on the remarkable resemblence. The mayor reciprocated with an even uglier potato-man. The cultural development strategy helped turn rivalry into co-operation, making 'The Ugly Potato-Man Festival' a bigger money-earner than Sydney's Gay & Lesbian Mardi Gra.

Where to from here?

Strategic plans are a necessary feature of contemporary organisational management. They can produce substantial and tangible benefits for organisations—providing they are well focused and are implemented conscientiously. Having made this commitment and the associated investment in people and resources, the effectiveness of your strategy should be monitored and your information database kept up-to-date. Shifts in demographic composition—more younger people, more older people, a larger Aboriginal or NESB community—may mean that policies and programs have to be modified from time to time. Your dynamic database can act as a performance indicator—indicating if your strategy is still relevant.

Subsequent revisions of your strategy should examine and rectify areas of the strategy that are not working and build upon the successful aspects. These annual reviews, scheduled in advance of the annual budgetary cycle, should include community consultation and be seen as an essential part of the ongoing implementation. Remember, however, that strategies are long term. Having spent 12 months carefully planning and shaping your strategy, you should resist the temptation to make unwarranted, drastic changes to it every year, just for the sake of doing something new. Be flexible and review things honestly, but retain your *strategic* focus and your future vision.

It is important to document your processes and the outcomes—including both your successes and failures. These can be published as booklets, videos, articles in professional journals or they can be packaged as presentations to conferences. Because cultural planning is such a new field, the sharing of information and experiences is essential for new understandings and practices to evolve and emerge. In this way the ripples of your cultural development strategy may impact on the wider Australian culture.

In 2044, Cr Jones looked down from his marble plinth. The sweat and toil had been worth it. He was now part of the cultural resources of Bulla Bulla—forever.

Appendix A
Facilitating small groups

What is facilitation?

There is a fundamental difference between *leading* a group and *facilitating*. Leading implies the destination is pre-determined. Facilitating, on the other hand, designs and manages a *process* which enables the group to make their own journey. In fact, a skilled facilitator, who does not have any content knowledge, can still ensure that an ideal outcome is achieved.

Facilitation involves:

- Designing an appropriate process to achieve the outcome desired by the group
- Observing what is happening or not happening in the group and highlighting this to the group
- Identifying and raising problems that are holding the group back
- Challenging inappropriate behaviour
- Drawing out ideas
- Getting to the bottom of objections
- Posing new approaches for problem solving.

The facilitation role is vital because once people are enmeshed in group activity, they become so absorbed in the content, they can miss process problems.

Why have a facilitator?

Working groups without a designated leader may find it difficult reaching a group decision. They may argue, go off on tangents, become involved in personality clashes, and lose all sense of a common goal. Disagreement and conflict are inevitably part of the group communication process. However, some of conflict is caused by factors which have nothing to do directly with the subject matter being discussed—some people take an instant dislike to each other, some may want to use the group process to further their own political agenda, or others may have had a fight with their partners on the way to the workshop. These are *extrinsic* conflicts, not directly related to the subject being discussed. On the other hand, *intrinsic* conflicts are related to the subject matter and are due to such things as contradictory evidence, differences in interpretation of facts, misunderstanding of ideas, differences in reasoning, or a different value system. Discussion can resolve these conflicts. The role of the facilitator is to moderate the extrinsic conflicts—which can't be resolved in the workshop—in order for the group to work through the intrinsic conflicts and arrive at a consensus.

What do facilitators do?

Facilitators anticipate the nature of the group and the group's likely attitudes to the subject matter—for example, is the community deeply divided or united on the issue? They find out what the topic is prior to the meeting and are informed on the substance of the issues. They take into account likely audience reaction. Is this a 'feel good' situation: for example, 'How do we improve our image,' or a threatening situation: for example, 'How do we manage eight months of highway construction through our town centre?'. They anticipate the manner, attitude, communication skills or other conditions of the participants.

Facilitators are willing to accept the customs and mores of the group without making value judgements. Facilitators put the group at ease and remove the barriers preventing people from contributing. They ease people into the group process by making sure everyone is acquainted. They see to it that the discussion gets off to a good start and that the participants are focused immediately on the problems and tasks at hand. They help the participants understand their function by explaining the purpose of the discussion and/or activities and correct any misconceptions.

Facilitators control and focus the direction of the discussion towards a specific goal. This channelling of the discussion is not leading the group to a predetermined set of statements, but helping them undertake the tasks necessary to reach a destination of their choosing. Nor does 'control' mean domination or manipulation of the group. Once the goal of the group process is established, the group often moves forward quite freely on its own. To restrict or to control in the traditional sense may stifle the free flow of information.

Facilitators create an atmosphere in which the participants feel understood and safe to communicate freely. The facilitator creates a comfortable physical environment—seating arranged so everyone is included; the potential for interruptions minimised; the ventilation and heating checked and drinking water available; and butchers paper and pens conveniently to hand. The facilitator must also create a positive attitudinal environment—a feeling that participants are free from serious threats to their egos. Participants need to feel that they can make contributions and that their integrity will be respected by other participants, and that the other participants will make a significant effort to understand what they are trying to say.

Facilitators should understand human emotions and stress. Sometimes participants may become emotionally involved in the process and actually criticise and attack the facilitator. The able facilitator avoids responding or buying into this conflict by recognising that this is not an attack on them personally.

A facilitator develops skill in the timing of questions and providing transitions. Just as a parent senses when a child needs help and when the child should be left to its own devices, a person skilled in timing has a sense of when to do or say something and when to let the group explore a side-track for a few moments. For example, sometimes people need to get something off their chest, even though it may be irrelevant, before they can focus on the task at hand.

The facilitator listens carefully. As a listener, the facilitator tunes in on at least three levels: *visually*, they observe the reactions of the participants; *aurally*, they hear what is being said; and *physically*, they demonstrate to the speaker they are listening by looking directly at them and adopting an 'I-am-listening-and-interested' pose.

The facilitator ensures that what is said is recorded accurately. Recording group discussions can help in building consensus. As the facilitator records, they should check that they have heard correctly and what they have written captures the full spirit and essential details of what has been said. Checking with the participants helps the facilitator correct any errors in understanding and reassures participants that their contributions are being taken seriously. The facilitator uses feedback frequently and effectively as a corrective device that allows both the speaker and the listener to check the degree to which the basic message has been received.

Processes of facilitation

- Introduce yourself and explain the role of a facilitator. Select a recorder. Review the responsibilities of the participants. Have each participant introduce themselves.
- Set the ground rules. 'Everyone is encouraged to be active. Participants should not interrupt each other. Comments should be limited to *x* minutes at a time.' Enforcement is much easier when ground rules are set at the start rather than after problems arise. Describe the timing of the session and breaks, and any other housekeeping details. Review the agenda for each session. Modify if necessary to accommodate the priorities of the group.

- Describe how the session will be conducted; what discussion techniques will be used, that is, free-for-all, brainstorming, round robin, parliamentary procedure, voting, mini-survey, panel discussion, consensus development, having each person write their opinions/ suggestions on an index card to be collected and shared with the group or scientific problem solving.
- Keep the sessions on schedule. Start on time. Stop on time.
- Keep the group to the agenda and the particular task before it. For example, 'Your comments are interesting, but we are getting off the original topic. Let's deal with one thing at a time'.
- Postpone proposing and discussing 'solutions' until the group has first agreed on the 'problem' to be solved and/or the desired outcome. Keep the group from getting bogged down on how to do it before they have agreed on what is to be accomplished.
- Probe deeply. Ask the same question around the group, either factual or perceptual. 'How would you rate that?' Make comparisons. 'Is A more important than B? Why or why not?' Probe experiences. 'Why don't you tell us about ...?' 'Does anyone else have a similar or widely different opinion?' Set up a situation. 'If ..., how do you think you would react?' Give a hypothetical task. 'You have been assigned to a task force to ..., how would you go about it?' 'Let's assume that you get notification that ..., what would you do with that, how would you handle it? What role would you play?'
- Maintain your credibility by strictly enforcing the agreed-upon ground rules in a consistent manner. Be firm but fair e.g. 'Linda, we agreed at the start of the meeting that we would ...'.
- Serve as a traffic cop in making sure that everyone has an equal opportunity to express their opinions and suggestions. If someone gets windy, interrupt with 'we appreciate and will take into consideration your comments, but let's allow others to express their views too'.
- Urge participants to express their opinions without judging or putting down the suggestions of others. Encourage 'I feel we should ...' statements rather than 'I disagree with ...' statements.

Stay positive. Ask those who are critical or negative how they would handle the problem—what would they recommend. This is a great way to diffuse negative vibes and force them to be pro-active.

- Show that you are listening and indicate that you appreciate each individual's input.

- Act as a mediator when conflicts arise. Stay neutral as much as possible. We cannot say that the facilitator should always maintain a certain objective distance from the group members. Sometimes a high level of interpersonal involvement is essential to reaching the necessary levels of acceptance that allow the participants to speak freely. However, when the facilitator is perceived as 'too close' a resistance to following group process may result or lack of objectivity may colour the results.

- When things bog down or problems arise, call for a *'stop session'*. A stop session is stopping a meeting for a couple of minutes to reflect on what is happening within the group. For example: 'I feel uncomfortable about ... How do the rest of you feel?' or 'Hey, the negativity in this room is tremendous. Let's take a look at it. What can we do about it?' Or: 'We seem to have reached a stand-off. Let's take a break and then come back and do some brainstorming. Maybe we can find another approach that would be acceptable to both sides'.

- Finally, success depends on the group. Remind the group that it is their meeting. If they don't like what is happening, they should say so and change it. As a facilitator, don't be afraid to ask the group for help. 'I don't quite know how to handle this. What approach do you think we should use? Does anyone have any suggestions?' If you let people know that you're trying your best and seek their assistance, they will be more tolerant of your mistakes and feel more responsible for what happens. You have to be sincere in your request and remain non-defensive if criticised.

Understanding group dynamics

Group formation

Groups go through a formation process. Some of the stages are slow, some are turbulent. All are appropriate, and like any pattern of development, are necessary to the healthy growth of a group. A skilled facilitator observes the stages as they occur, understands their intrinsic worth, and works with the group to move appropriately through the stages.

The first stage is *forming*. When a group first meets, people are cautious and want to get to know each other. They are tentative and tend to check each other out. Generally they are polite, but somewhat reserved, and offer little argument. This can be a slow stage, especially if members feel uncomfortable with each other or the task that they are to deal with or if they believe there are hidden agendas in the group. To assist the formation stage, a facilitator needs to provide a safe environment for the group to operate in and to set goals for the groups to achieve.

Process steps which will ensure that the group doesn't get stuck in this phase include: provide adequate getting-to-know-you time; allow people an opportunity to share hopes and concerns; and pace the group appropriately so that they move through this stage easily. If some members get stuck here they may keep quiet because they don't feel comfortable airing their views.

The second stage is *storming*. This can be an openly tempestuous time where members challenge each other and the facilitator for dominance and/or air time. Storming can also be a time where quiet subversiveness is used to challenge ideas or to establish dominance. This is the stage least liked by most people. Yet, it is an extremely productive time. When there is no storming, often the most dominant group members will push the group their way, and many good ideas lost. The group can meander and lose heart. During this stage, a facilitator watches for blatant or surreptitious storming and deals with it so all get air time, no idea is pushed aside too quickly, and personality differences are acknowledged in a non-destructive manner. People should be encouraged to express their feelings, but at times the facilitator may need to remind the group about the ground rules and agreed goals.

The third stage is *norming*. During this stage, group members will begin to establish their purpose and will subtly or blatantly develop rules for behaviour during the life of the group. Norming is important. It is a time when cohesiveness and mutual support forms. People show that they are willing to consider alternative ideas and opinions and will negotiate and debate willingly. There is a lot of sharing of ideas, feelings, history and hopes. Friendly joking is common at this stage.

If norming does not occur, group functioning can become confused and some members may withdraw. Actions that will help a group through this stage are:

- Encourage other group members to take on some of the jobs that you normally do
- Encourage people to suggest different ways of doing things.
- Support new ideas and constructive argument and disagreement within the group.

The fourth stage is *performing*. During this stage, the group settles into achieving its objectives in a collective manner. This is usually the time when the group achieves its goal. During this time, encourage full involvement, acceptance of other views, voluntary effort, warm relationships within the group and creativity. Don't interfere; do affirm the quality of individual and group effort, delegate, take on new challenges and, most importantly, celebrate success.

The final stage is called *mourning*. Every group ceases to meet because the task has been completed. A well-established group which has enjoyed sharing success may now suffer a sense of loss. A facilitator needs to help the group establish a new task, a new role if that is appropriate. If not, the facilitator can help the group mourn its loss by talking things through or organising a social function a month or so ahead.

Group roles

Belbin discovered that people have one or two preferred roles when working in groups. Many problems in groups emerge because a number of people are vying to play the same role or because no one fulfils a particular role. If the group is going round in circles, it is usually because no one is filling a directive role or that no one is filling a finisher role. If a group lacks creativity, it is usually because the group lacks an originator or two who can come up with good ideas. When a group is experiencing difficulties related to roles, it is sometimes appropriate to explain the need for a full range of roles and suggest that someone change roles.

Behaviours which help and hinder group effectiveness

A facilitator needs to encourage appropriate behaviour and discourage the inappropriate. *Task* behaviours are useful to groups because they move the group towards achieving its objectives. *Maintenance* behaviours satisfy the emotional needs of group members in order to maintain group cohesion and stability. *Idiosyncratic* behaviours are used to satisfy an individual's personal needs in ways which do not contribute to the group's objectives.

Task behaviours include:

- *Initiating activity*—proposing solutions, suggesting new ideas, providing new definitions to the problem, new attacks on problems or new organisation of material
- *Information seeking*—asking for clarification of suggestions, requesting additional information or facts
- *Information giving*—offering facts, generalisations, or personal anecdotes
- *Opinion giving*—stating an opinion or belief based on personal values about established facts

- *Elaborating*—clarifying by giving examples or developing meanings, trying to envisage how a proposal might work out if it is adopted
- *Coordinating*—showing relationships among various ideas or suggestions, trying to pull ideas and suggestions together, trying to draw together activities of various sub-groups or members
- *Summarising*—pulling together related ideas or suggestions, restating suggestions after the group has discussed them
- *Testing feasibility*—making application of suggestions to real situations, examining practicality and workability of ideas, evaluating possible decisions
- *Evaluating*—submitting group decisions or accomplishments to comparison with group standards, measuring accomplishments against goals
- *Diagnosing*—determining sources of difficulties and the main blocks to progress; suggesting next appropriate step.

Maintenance behaviours include:

- *Encouraging*—being friendly, warm and responsive to others, praising others and their ideas, agreeing with and accepting contributions of others
- *Gate keeping*—trying to make it possible for another member to make a contribution to the group, suggesting limited talking time for everyone so that everyone will have a chance to be heard
- *Standard setting*—expressing standards for the group to use in choosing its content or procedures or in evaluating its decisions, reminding the group to avoid decisions which conflict with group's standards
- *Following*—going along with decisions of the group, somewhat persuasively accepting ideas of others, serving audience during group discussion and decision making
- *Expressing group feeling*—sensing and summarising group feelings, describing group reactions to ideas or solutions

- *Consensus taking*—tentatively asking for group opinions in order to find out if the group is nearing consensus for a decision, sending up 'trial balloons' to test group opinions
- *Harmonising*—mediating, conciliating differences in points of view, making compromise solutions
- *Tension reducing*—draining off negative feelings by jesting or pouring oil on troubled waters, putting a tense situation into a wider context.

Idiosyncratic behaviours include:

- *Aggression*—working for status by criticising or blaming others, showing hostility against the group or some individual, deflating the ego or status of others
- *Blocking*—interfering with the progress of the group by going off in a tangent citing personal experiences unrelated to the problem, arguing too much on a point, rejecting ideas without consideration
- *Self-confessing*—using the group as a dumping ground for personal feelings or points of view which are not oriented to the group
- *Competing*—vying with others to produce the best ideas, talk the most, play the most roles, gain force with leader
- *Seeking sympathy*—trying to induce other group members to be sympathetic to one's problems or misfortunes, deploring one's own ideas to gain support
- *Special pleading*—introducing or supporting suggestions related to one's own pet concerns or philosophies, lobbying
- *Horsing around*—clowning, joking, mimicking, disrupting
- *Recognition seeking*—attempting to call attention to one's self by loud or excessive talking, extreme ideas, or unusual behaviour
- *Withdrawing*—acting indifferently, passive, resorting to excessive formality, daydreaming, doodling, whispering to others, wandering from the subject.

Experience shows people tend to prefer to use *either* task or maintenance behaviours. Groups which have one or two maintenance people tend to run more smoothly and reach decisions quicker than groups whose make-up is predominantly task-oriented. A facilitator needs to be able to identify behaviours, which, although culturally acceptable, cause the group to dysfunction. Once identified, these behaviours need to be challenged in a manner which assists the person to develop more appropriate methods of behaviour. It should also be noted that extreme use of either task or maintenance behaviours can also be dysfunctional to a group. A facilitator needs to exercise judgement as to what balance of behaviours is acceptable to achieving the group objectives.

Groupthink

Generally in our culture, conflict is viewed as negative and to be avoided. (Conflict is usually a positive force, but if unharnessed, becomes destructive.) Facilitators therefore often place considerable emphasis on managing conflict. However, this can produce an even more destructive phenomenon—*groupthink*. Groupthink is where all conflict is avoided by a group in order to achieve cohesiveness and unanimity. The group fails to think creatively or realistically appraise alternative courses of action.

To avoid groupthink, a facilitator needs to watch for: discussion limited to few alternative courses of action; selective bias in the way the group reacts to information from specialists and other outside critics; self-censoring; or shared stereotypes in which there is a tendency to regard the 'opposition' as stupid or uninformed. Groups experiencing groupthink will share an illusion of morality or inherent rightness.

To minimise groupthink, a facilitator needs to challenge any group insularity, avoid over-directive leadership practices, and guard against premature consensus.

Getting the most out of groups

The success of working groups is largely dependent on the quality of group interaction. The people assigned to your group will come from a variety of professional and social backgrounds. As a group they bring a vast amount of experience and knowledge that is a valuable resource. Because of diverse personalities, each will have a contribution to make to group processes. To get the most out of a group:

- Encourage by praising ideas. Body language, such as nodding your head, is important.
- Mediate the viewpoints of group members by offering compromises. Sometimes rephrasing the opposing viewpoints will help resolve conflicts.
- Provide opportunities for all members to contribute to the discussion, even if it means blocking an over-zealous member. Change the focus by asking another participant to comment on the point just made. Go around the group and ask each person to react to the point at hand
- Avoid putting people reticent to speak on the spot. Give them advance warning that you are going to ask their opinion.
- Summarise periodically to keep the group on the point and to suggest what steps should be taken next.
- Accept the group's decision even if it's not what you had in mind. If their conclusions are based on incorrect information, give them the right information.
- Lighten up the discussion with humour if the situation becomes tense.
- Diagnose problems without singling out any individual. Offer suggestions for how to step beyond the problem.
- Involve the whole group in censoring a participant who is disruptive and has not responded to more subtle attempts to moderate behaviour. As a last resort the group can vote to restrict or silence the offender.

• Accept the conclusions of the group and report them faithfully. You can add to their conclusions, but do not make the group feel that their work was inadequate or irrelevant.

To summarise, here are ten golden rules for facilitators:

• Obtain agreement on ground rules at the beginning of discussion.

• Provide a relaxed atmosphere, encouraging humour and good fellowship.

• Allow for open discussion while maintaining a focus.

• Encourage involvement of all participants and prevent dominance by a few.

• Praise and probe.

• Monitor the environment to ensure the physical comfort of participants.

• Avoid leading participants to a predetermined outcome.

• Assist the participants in summarising their discussion.

• Bring closure on topics discussed.

• Serve as the moderator—not a participant—of the discussion.

Appendix B

Livability resources and indicators

Nature of livability resources

There are tangible community assets—*livability resources*—that contribute to quality of life. Personal income is a livability resource, but only one among many. In chapter 4, two of these livability resources were discussed in some depth—the *altruistic surplus* and *creative wealth*.

One example given of the altruistic surplus was Portland where residents have raised money, with no help from government, to progressively buy pieces of bushland to be preserved as an environmental park. The high level of citizen involvement in enhancing the city is what makes Portland stand out in contrast to many other US cities.

To try and put an economic price on Portland's altruistic surplus is to denigrate the very nature of this resource: it is an activity which is *not* motivated by economic imperatives. It is true that this altruistic surplus has an economic benefit. It improves the livability of the city which makes the city more attractive for businesses, attracts tourists, etc. But this is just one of the side-benefits of the altruistic surplus.

The altruistic surplus also promotes feelings of self-esteem, belonging and 'value to significant others'. Money cannot buy any of these. Therefore the altruistic surplus, like many other livability resources, are *'non-pricable'* commodities.

Planning must take account of how its proposals impact on the full range of livability resources. It must also take account of *livability corrosives*—elements that attack and destroy livability resources, for example, fear of crime or noise pollution. Cultural planning, together with all other forms of planning, needs the following three levels of information:

- *Livability resources and livability corrosives:* What is the full range of livability resources and livability corrosives? Resources, such as the altruistic surplus, or children's independent mobility, or the walkability of neighbourhoods, are tangible assets that can be built up or diminished. Governments and industry should be accountable for the management of these resources. Corrosives are also tangible commodities that can be increased or decreased.

- *Livability indicators:* How do we measure the health or otherwise of livability resources? An indicator is 'a pointing device... an instrument which indicates the condition of a machine' (Macquarie Dictionary). Livability indicators are signposts or measures that indicate the levels and conditions (health) of the city's livability resources. Similarly, levels of the corrosive factors can also be measured.

- *Livability benchmarks:* A benchmark is 'a point of reference from which quality of excellence is measured' (Macquarie Dictionary) The levels of acceptable air or water pollution set by the World Health Organisation are a benchmark relating to a livability resource against which authorities can measure their performance and against which they can set policy and program goals.

International studies

Glasgow perceptual indicators

In 1988 the *Glasgow Quality of Life Group* and *Allied Population Research Unit* at the University of Glasgow surveyed 1403 people from 38 major UK cities, asking them to rank 19 perceptual indicators of quality of life on a scale of 1 to 5. The results, summarised in figure B.1, show that only one economic indicator—cost of living—figured

Dimension	Weighting on a scale of 1-5
Violent crime	3.709
Non-violent crime	3.693
Health provision	3.633
Pollution levels	3.407
Cost of living *	3.390
Shopping facilities	3.308
Access to areas of scenic quality	3.007
Cost of owner occupied housing*	2.992
Education provision	2.869
Employment prospects*	2.826
Wage levels	2.822
Unemployment levels*	2.729
Climate	2.638
Sports facilities	2.629
Travel to work times	2.516
Leisure facilities	2.477
Quality of council housing	2.204
Access to council housing*	2.045
Cost of private rented accommodation*	1.916

*Economic indicators

Figure B.1 *The* Glasgow Perceptual Indicators *average weightings of the dimensions of quality of life, in order of perceived importance to the average person*

in the top six. Employment prospects, wage levels and unemployment levels came in at positions 10, 11 and 12. This research indicates that the quality-of-life issues are assuming a much higher level of importance on the political agenda.

Oregon benchmarks

The *Oregon Benchmarks* grew directly out of *Oregon Shines,* a 20-year strategic vision developed in 1989 with strong citizen participation. The purpose of the benchmarks 'is to guide our state to a better future as a people, as a place, and as an economy' (Oregon Progress Board, 1991: p1). The 272 benchmarks are 'outcome focused', aimed at measuring results rather than programs or expenditure. The benchmarks are grouped into three basic categories:

* Exceptional people
* Outstanding quality of life
* Diverse, robust economy.

The benchmarks were all designed to be measured historically (in the years 1970,1980 and 1990) and then targets were set as policy objectives for the years 1995, 2000 and 2010. They were also prioritised to the extent that a number of benchmarks were identified as 'critical'. These were further categorised as:

* *Lead benchmarks*: short-term problem areas where improvements are required within a 5-year timeframe
* *Key benchmarks*: fundamental, long term areas where solid performance is necessary to ongoing quality of life.

The benchmarks are recognition that one of the by-products of the specialised society is that specialists lose sight of the 'big picture' and the means become the end. The benchmarks are an attempt to get bureaucracies to focus on the goal rather than the means. The major difficulty with the Oregon Benchmarks is that there is some confusion between *indicators* and *benchmarks*. However, it is a significant shift to a more holistic form of planning.

A preliminary list

Figure B.2 is a preliminary listing of *livability resources* and *livability corrosives* drawn from *Livability Technology & Traffic Reduction* (Engwicht 1994). It is illustrative rather than comprehensive or definitive.

KEY: Items not indented are a livability resource or corrosive. The items marked ❱ are indicators or potential ways of measuring that resource or corrosive.

LIVABILITY RESOURCES

Altruistic surplus
- ❱ Hours spent in voluntary community service
- ❱ Percentage of income donated to community organisations
- ❱ Percentage of the population not maximising their income so they can spend time building relationships or serving the community

Creative wealth
- ❱ Percentage of business income going to R&D
- ❱ Percentage of population working full time on creative activities
- ❱ Percentage of population working part-time on creative activities
- ❱ Percentage of population with cross-social/cultural friendships
- ❱ Measures of creative output (books, films, plays etc.)

Confidence/flexibility
- ❱ Business confidence
- ❱ Self-confidence as measured by level of confidence that a person would survive/thrive if certain life situations changed or they were presented with particular challenges (lose job, become disabled, asked to run the city, etc.)

Independent mobility
- ❱ At what age are children given certain 'licences' for independent mobility? (Paul Tranter 1993)
- ❱ What are the 'exchange rates' for those without constant access to a car—particularly for older people, women, children and those with disabilities—compared to those with constant access?
- ❱ Transportation choices—modes available and flexibility

Figure B:2. A preliminary list of livability resources and corrosives. Cont.>

Accessibility

▶ Perceived ease of reaching a number of archetypical journey ends (e.g. corner store, cinema, chemist, doctor, library, etc.) by foot, cycle, public transport and private motor vehicle

Walkability

▶ Children's independent mobility
▶ Perceived accessibility
▶ Number of public sitting spots per household
▶ Chances of meeting someone while walking
▶ Women's rating of neighbourhood safety
▶ Continuity and quality of footpaths

Exchange facilitation environment

▶ *Exchange rates*—Total number of exchanges, planned and spontaneous, transacted per person per day
▶ *Exchange efficiency*—Cost per exchange: economic, environmental, resources (energy and time) and social

Exchange equity

▶The *exchange rates* for children, women, those without access to a car and those with disabilities expressed as a percentage of the average exchange rates

Placemaking resources

▶ The number of the following archetypical placemaking elements that residents feel they have access to. Places that:

• draw you out of a preoccupation with the present and mundane
• evoke a feeling of connection to city and neighbourhood past
• evoke a feeling of connection to family and personal past
• evoke a feeling of connection to existing community
• evoke feelings of connection to nature
• evoke feelings of 'ecstatic exuberance'—celebration, play, aliveness
• evoke a sense of mystery and adventure
• 'secret places'—private places for reflection and daydreaming
• confront and provoke
• create opportunity for 'people watching'.

Scenic quality
Climate
Education
Diversity of goods and services

Figure B:2 cont.>

Physical health
- Life expectancy
- Fitness levels
- Incidence of preventable diseases

Emotional health
- Suicide rates
- Mental illness rates
- Perceptions of 'inner contentment'

Tolerance
- Levels of hate crimes
- Perceptions of acceptance and support by minority groups

Personal growth infrastructure
- Perceptions of community support in times of need, and in pursuing personal growth
- Levels of cultural and social infrastructure

Accessibility to decision making
- Perceptions of ability to influence decision making
- Percentage of people with direct lines of communication to decision-makers

Meaningful work
- Employment/unemployment rates
- Degree of support for those pursuing non-traditional work (artists, thinkers, social reformers, etc.)
- Perceptions of this degree of support
- Perceptions of degree of control in workplace
- Levels of work satisfaction

Integrated diversity
- Diversity of industry
- Community and cultural diversity
- Number of meaningful interpersonal exchanges between people of different social and cultural backgrounds
- Number of 'hate' crimes

Personal income
- Employment prospects
- Purchasing power of average income
- Income distribution

Figure B:2 cont.>

Social equity
- Income distribution
- Percentage of those with disabilities in meaningful employment
- Exchange rates for different groups

LIVABILITY CORROSIVES
Energy and resource deficit
- Levels of consumption of non-renewable energy and resources per person

Crime rates
- Real
- Perceived

Fear
- Differential between real and perceived crime rates
- Perceptions that 'something bad will happen to me in the next...'

Pollution
- Non-recyclable rubbish and pollutants produced per person
- Air and water quality

Excessive noise

Homelessness

Life-years wasted
- Life-years lost via accidents, suicide, preventable disease

Figure B.2 A preliminary list of livability resources and corrosives

Appendix C

Going further–
helpful resources

The bibliography contains a wide range of texts. Cultural planning is a method of viewing our living environments holistically. If you would like to find out more about how all the elements of our living environment are intimately interconnected, a good place to start is: *The death and life of great American cities,* Jane Jacobs, 1961; *The experience of place,* Tony Hiss, 1990; *City of Quartz,* Mike Davis, 1990; *Towards an eco-city,* Engwicht, 1991; *Streets for people,* Rudofsky, 1969; *Discovering the vernacular landscape,* John Jackson, 1984; or *A pattern language,* Christopher Alexander et al.

If you are looking for 'how-to' books, there are a large number in the bibliography.

Perhaps the most valuable listing of resources is contained in the Australia Council/Envirobook publication *Places not spaces: placemaking in Australia.* (Winikoff 1995) The first part of the book gives an introduction to the concepts of placemaking and then documents a range of ground-breaking projects around Australia—complete with colour photos. The last part of the book gives comprehensive listings of:

- Information sources for each state with all contact details including phone and fax numbers. Covers government departments, agencies, funding sources, tertiary institutions and community-based organisations
- Books and publications—many with a summary
- Journals, catalogues and reports
- Videos and slide-kits.

Select Bibliography

Alexander, et al. 1977 *A pattern language: towns, buildings, construction*, Oxford University Press, New York.

Appleyard, Donald. 1981 *Livable streets*, University of Californian Press, Berkeley.

Australian Bureau of Statistics. 1992 *A guide to Australian social statistics*, Australian Bureau of Statistics.

Australian Local Government Association. 1993 *A guide to integrated planning*, ALGA, Canberra.

Bianchini, Franco, et al.1989 *City centres, city cultures*, Comedia, London, and Centre for Local Economic Strategies, Manchester.

Bianchini, Franco. *Urban cultural policy in Britain and Europe: towards cultural planning*, Institute for Cultural Policy Studies, Griffith University, Brisbane.

Bonnin, Roberta. 1993 *The festivals review*, Arts Queensland, Brisbane.

Brecknock, Richard., 1992 'Public art—public places—public money', *Culture and Policy* Vol. 4. Institute for Cultural Policy Studies, Griffith University, Brisbane.

Community Health Research Unit. 1991 *Planning healthy communities, a guide to doing community needs assessment*, Flinders Press.

Cunningham, Chris. 1994 *Towards a new planning framework: a philosophical response to David Engwicht's proposal*, unpublished paper.

Cutler, Laurence Stephan & Cutler, Sherrie Stephens. 1977 'Establishing a dialogue for recycling cities' *Ekistics*, 256 March 1977, 165–171.

Davis, Mike. 1990 *City of quartz: excavating the future in Los Angeles*. Vintage, London.

de Bono, Edward. 1991 *I am right, you are wrong—from this to the new renaissance: from rock logic to water logic* Penguin, London.

Dick, Bob. 1987 *Helping groups to be effective: skills, processes and concepts for group facilitation*, Interchange, Brisbane.

Donovan, Andrew. 1993 *Creative councils, the South Australian arts and local government consultancy project*, Local Government Association of South Australia, Adelaide.

Engwicht, David. 1992 *Towards an eco-city: calming the traffic*. Envirobook, Sydney. (Published 1993 in USA and Canada as *Reclaiming our cities and towns: living better with less traffic*. New Society Publishers, Philadelphia.)

—— *Finding the personality of our place: towards a cultural development strategy—Report 1*, Maroochy Shire Council, Nambour.

Glasgow University Quality of Life Group. 1989 *Qualify of life in Britain's towns and cities*, Glasgow.

Fleming, R.L. & von Tscharner, R. 1981 *Placemakers: public art that tells you where you are*, MA: Hastings House, Cambridge.

Hall, Peter. 1992 *Cities of tomorrow: an intellectual history of urban planning and design in the twentieth century*, Basil Blackwell, Oxford.

Hillier, Bill & Hanson, Julienne. 1990 *The social logic of space*. Cambridge University Press, Cambridge.

Hillier, Bill. 1992 'Milton Keynes: look back to London' *AJ 15 April*. pp. 42–46.

Hiss, Tony. 1990 *The experience of place: a new way of looking at and dealing with our radically changing cities and countryside*, Vintage Books, New York.

Jackson, John Brickerhoff. 1984 *Discovering the vernacular landscape.* Yale University Press, New Haven.

Jacobs, Jane. 1961 *The death and life of great American cities.* Random House, New York.

Kreisberg, Luisa. 1979 *Local government and the arts*, American Council for the Arts, New York.

Lewers Bequest and Penrith Regional Art Gallery. 1993 *Hypothetically Public.* Emu Plains.

McNulty, Robert. 1989 'The economics of amenity', *Meanjin, 4.*

Mercer, Colin. 1992 'Brisbane's cultural development strategy: the process, the politics and the product' *Artwork*, Community Arts Network of South Australia.

Mulgan, Geoff & Worpole, Ken. 1986 *Saturday night or Sunday morning? From arts to industry—new forms of cultural policy*, Comedia, London.

Newman, Peter. 1975 'An ecological model for city structure and development' *Ekistics 239*, October 1975, pp. 258–265.

Office of Local Government. 1988 *A guide to community needs assessment*, Australian Government Publishing Service, Canberra.

Oregon Progress Board. 1991*Oregon benchmarks: standards for measuring statewide progress and government performance—report to the 1991 Oregon Legislature*, Salem, Oregon.

Roberts, Jean. 1989, 'Local government and community development', *Australian local government handbook*, Commonwealth of Australia, AGPS, Canberra.

Rudofsky, Bernard. 1969 *Streets for people: a primer for Americans*, Doubleday & Company, New York.

Scott, C. 1989 'Cultural planning and cultural tourism, models for community control and development' *Museums Quarterly News*, Nos. 3–4.

Sennett, Richard. 1990 *The conscience of the eye: the design and social life of cities*, Alfred A. Knopf, New York.

Snedcof, Harvey. 1984 *Cultural facilities in mixed use development*, Urban Land Institute, Washington, DC.

Sansom, Graham. 1992 *Making the connections: towards integrated local area planning*. Australian Local Government Association, Canberra.

Schneider, Kenneth R. 1979 *On the nature of cities*. Jossey-Bass Publication, San Francisco.

Stevens, Louise. 1990 *Community cultural planning kit*, University of Massachusetts, Massachusetts.

Stevenson, D. 1992 'Urban re-enchantment and the magic of cultural planning' *Culture and Policy*, Vol. 4. Institute for Cultural Policy Studies, Griffith University, Brisbane.

Tanghe, Jan, Vlaeminck, Sieg & Berghoef, Jo. 1984 *Living cities*. Pergamon Press, Oxford.

Tranter, P.J. 1993 *Children's mobility in Canberra: confinement or independence?* Monograph Series No. 7, Department of Geography Oceanography, Australian Defence Force Academy, Canberra.

Violette, C. & Taqqu, R. (eds) 1982 *Issues in supporting the arts*, Graduate School of Business and Public Administration, Cornell University, Ithaca.

Wates, N. and Knelt, C. 1987 *Community architecture: how people are creating their own environment*, Penguin, London.

Watson, Sophie. 1992 'Contested spaces: cross-cultural issues in planning' *Culture and Policy*, Vol. 4. Institute for Cultural Policy Studies, Griffith University, Brisbane.

Wildman, Paul. 1992 *Action learning and community economic development*, Prosperity Press.

Wildman, Paul & Hubley, Gavin. 1993 *The use of process management in sustainable community economic development*, Prosperity Press.

Wildman, Paul & Wilson, Peter. 1993 *Helping organisations think creatively: the clever country revisited*, Prosperity Press.

Winikoff, Tamara (ed.). 1995 *Places not spaces: placemaking in Australia*, Envirobook, Sydney.

Worpole, Ken. 1992 *Towns for people: transforming urban life*, Open University Press, Milton Keynes.

Whyte, William H. 1980 *The social life of small urban spaces.* Conservation Foundation, Washington, DC.

Zukin, Sharon. 1982 *Loft living: culture and capital in urban change*, Johns Hopkins University Press, Baltimore.

—— 1991 *Lanscapes of power: from Detroit to Disneyland*, University of California Press, Berkeley.

Index

A

B

C

Printed in Great Britain
by Amazon.co.uk, Ltd.,
Marston Gate.